TALES OF ANCIENT PERSIA

Oxford Myths and Legends
in paperback

*

African Myths and Legends
Kathleen Arnott

Armenian Folk-tales and Fables
Charles Downing

Chinese Myths and Fantasies
Cyril Birch

English Fables and Fairy Stories
James Reeves

French Legends, Tales and Fairy Stories
Barbara Leonie Picard

Hungarian Folk-tales
Val Biro

Indian Tales and Legends
J E B Gray

Japanese Tales and Legends
Helen and William McAlpine

Tales of Ancient Persia
Barbara Leonie Picard

Russian Tales and Legends
Charles Downing

Scandinavian Legends and Folk-tales
Gwyn Jones

Scottish Folk-tales and Legends
Barbara Ker Wilson

West Indian Folk-tales
Philip Sherlock

The Iliad
Barbara Leonie Picard

The Odyssey
Barbara Leonie Picard

Gods and Men
John Bailey, Kenneth McLeish,
David Spearman

Tales of Ancient Persia

Retold from the Shah-Nāma *of Firdausi*

by

BARBARA
LEONIE PICARD

Illustrated by

VICTOR G AMBRUS

OXFORD UNIVERSITY PRESS

OXFORD NEW YORK TORONTO

Oxford University Press, Walton Street, Oxford OX2 6DP

Oxford New York Toronto
Delhi Bombay Calcutta Madras Karachi
Kuala Lumpur Singapore Hong Kong Tokyo
Nairobi Dar es Salaam Cape Town
Melbourne Auckland Madrid

and associated companies in
Berlin Ibadan

Oxford is a trade mark of Oxford University Press

First published 1972
First published in paperback 1993

A CIP catalogue record for this book is available from the British Library

ISBN 0 19 274154 3

Printed in Great Britain
on acid-free paper

Contents

Preface

THE stories retold here are all taken from the *Shah-Nāma*—the King-Book—a very long epic poem by the great Iranian poet Firdausi, which gives the history of his country from the Creation down to its conquest by the Arabs in the seventh century. None of the stories is Firdausi's own invention; he himself retold them all from the myths and early legendary history of Iran. Roughly, the first half of the *Shah-Nāma* tells of mythical and legendary kings and heroes, and the second half tells of historical personages—though many of the exploits of these latter, as given by Firdausi, have little basis in fact. In this selection, the stories are all taken from the first, legendary, half of the poem.

Little is known of the life of Abul Kasim Mansur, whose pen-name was Firdausi; though, since he has always been reckoned the greatest of the Iranian poets, several colourful tales have gathered about his name. He was born around A.D. 940 and died in A.D. 1020. He began the *Shah-Nāma* when he was in middle age, and it took him thirty-five years to complete. There is a tradition that he wrote the *Shah-Nāma* for his patron, the Sultan Mahmud of Ghazni, in order to provide a dowry for his only daughter. But when the poem was finally completed, the Sultan cheated Firdausi, giving him only 60,000 silver coins instead of the 60,000 gold pieces he had promised. Firdausi, very angry, wrote a bitter satire on Mahmud and fled from Ghazni. The story goes on to tell how, some ten or twelve years later, the Sultan Mahmud repented of his meanness and sent to Firdausi either the gold he owed or its equivalent in precious indigo. But it was too late. The Sultan's messenger arrived at the moment that Firdausi's body was being carried to burial. It is said that Firdausi's daughter, with fine pride, spurned the Sultan's belated gift, and the money was used to found a hospice for the poor.

Firdausi himself, like his Iranian contemporaries, was a Mohammedan; but the characters and events of the *Shah-Nāma* are all from pre-Islamic sources. The Persians in the *Shah-Nāma* are not the Mohammedans of medieval and modern Iran, they are the ancestors of the ancient Persians who followed the dualistic religion taught by Zoroaster; those Persians who were defeated by the Greeks at Salamis and Marathon, and who were conquered by Alexander the Great; those Persians whose Great King Xerxes was probably the Ahasuerus of the Bible who married the Jewess Esther in the Old Testament story; the Persians of the wide empire of Darius, whose language was pure Indo-European, uninfluenced by Arabic.

Those hereditary enemies of the Persians in the *Shah-Nāma*, whom I have here called the Turanians, were perhaps originally a local tribe which resisted early Persian conquest, and whose resistance was magnified to symbolize the eternal struggle of evil against good: Ahrimān—sometimes called Angra Mainyu—against Ormuzd—also called Ahura Mazda. In later times Turān was usually equated with the Turkish empire.

No one particular form of transliteration of Arabic script has been used consistently for the proper names in this book. Instead, in each individual case I have used that form which I considered would be the best known to the reader. As regards pronunciation, the vowels should be as in Italian, with ā as the long 'a' in 'father'.

1: The Earliest Kings

In the very beginning of things, Ormuzd, who is goodness and light, created the world and all that is good and beautiful in the universe. But for everything to which Ormuzd gave being, Ahrimān, who is darkness and evil, created an opposite. Against love he set hatred; against joy, sorrow; to destroy peace, he made war; he formed demons to defy the good spirits; death to end life; and so with all things that are. And Ahrimān it was who put falsehood and deceit in the minds of men where once there had been only the truth of Ormuzd.

The first king was named Keyumars and he reigned over the whole world. He dwelt in the mountains and wore the skins of leopards and he ruled justly and well. His people lived on the wild fruits which they picked and the roots which they pulled up, and they wore garments of leaves and were happy. But their happiness was not the will of Ahrimān, father of all ill, and he sent the Black Demon to make war upon Keyumars. In a terrible battle the Black Demon slew Siyāmek, Keyumars' brave son, and with his death it seemed as though the evil of Ahrimān would triumph for ever in the world.

But old King Keyumars sent for Husheng, the young son of Siyāmek, whom he loved greatly, and he said to him, 'It is you and I who must strive against the Black Demon, now that Siyāmek is no more. I will call together all who will fight for us and you shall have command of them.' He summoned to him all his people, and all those good spirits who lived in the world; together with the fierce, brave beasts of the wilderness, the leopards and the lions and the tigers; and all the birds of the air; and the kindly, tame, grass-eating beasts, the ox and the ass and the noble horse; and this army he gave into the charge of Husheng, to whom he said, 'With the help of great Ormuzd we shall be victorious and there will be peace in the world once again. But I do not think that I shall live to enjoy that peace. When I am dead, son of my son, my crown and my throne and my kingly power shall be yours. Rule well and justly, as I have ever striven to do.'

With Husheng at its head and old Keyumars leading the rear-guard, the army of men and animals and good spirits went forth hopefully. The Black Demon saw it come and with his horde of

lesser demons and evil spirits he rushed forward to the attack in a great cloud of dust that reached to the sky. After a fearful battle which shook the world, Husheng flung down the Black Demon, cut off his head and trampled upon his body, crying out in triumph;

and those demons and evil spirits who had not been slain fled, vanquished for a time.

His son avenged, Keyumars died, and Husheng set the crown on his head and sat upon the throne in his grandfather's place, and so began his rule of the world.

In Husheng's reign mankind prospered. He built channels and ditches to water the land and taught men to grow crops, so that they no longer depended solely upon wild fruits and roots for their nourishment. And he discovered iron in the mountains and separated it from the rocks in which it was hidden, so that his people might fashion tools for the cutting of timber and the tilling of the soil. And in Husheng's reign fire came to mankind.

This is the manner of that coming. One day as Husheng travelled through the world, from behind a mountain boulder a huge monster stepped into his path. It was long and it moved swiftly; its eyes were like two pools of blood, and it breathed out black smoke from its gaping mouth. Husheng's followers fled in terror, but the brave king stood firm. From the ground at his feet he picked up a piece of rock streaked with iron and cast it at the monster, which leapt aside. The stone struck against the boulder and a spark flew from it. The monster escaped unharmed; but Husheng made no attempt to pursue it. It was quite forgotten as he marvelled at what he had that moment learnt: that from the striking of iron against stone, a spark is born. And so, by the grace of Ormuzd, was fire given to Husheng and his people. By means of fire they could warm themselves in winter, and cook the roots and berries they ate, and bake bread from the crops they grew, and smelt iron. Fire, that shining blessing which raises men above the beasts, became for them a bright symbol of Ormuzd the good, and they worshipped it for the benefits it brought them.

After Husheng, the world was ruled by his son, Tahmuras the demon-binder, who fought successfully against the hosts of Ahrimān when they once more attacked mankind. And after Tahmuras came his son Jemshid. From the iron which his grandfather Husheng had taught men to mine from the rocks, Jemshid forged not only tools, but weapons of war—swords and spears, arrow-heads and coats of mail—to use in battle against the demons; and many victories over the evil beings who fought for Ahrimān did mankind celebrate because of these iron weapons. Yet not only the crafts of war, but those of peace also, did men learn under Jemshid, for he it was who first discovered for his people the arts of spinning and weaving, so that they could clothe themselves in garments of wool and silk and linen. He forced captive demons to serve him, making bricks from clay and building houses in which men might dwell, and raising stout walls to encircle the houses and protect them from attack. From plants he drew healing drugs to relieve the pain and sickness sent by Ahrimān. Ships he built, that men might sail from one part of the world to another. And then, when all the useful arts were in the possession of his subjects, Jemshid turned his thoughts to the arts of luxury. From the rocks he cut gems and precious marbles for jewellery and decoration, from fragrant flowers he distilled rich perfumes, and he had gold and silver wrought into adornments. And so daily his people praised him for all which he had taught them, and for all the benefits that he had bestowed on them.

But in time, with all the praise and gratitude men offered him, forgetting that without the will of Ormuzd no learning, no crafts and no benefits would have been possible, Jemshid became idle, vain, and proud, considering himself as great a benefactor to his people as divine Ormuzd. Not content with voyaging in a ship around the world he ruled, he ordered to be fashioned for himself a throne of gold and turquoise on which he sat in splendour to be carried through the air by winged demon slaves, as though he were the sun itself passing from end to end of the sky.

The days and the years passed and Jemshid grew in arrogance until he fancied himself greater than Ormuzd. He called all his lords and subject-kings together and spoke to them, saying, 'There is no other master of the universe beside myself. From me all gifts have come to you, my people, and it is I only whom you should worship. Bow down to me, not as to your king, but as to the creator of the universe.'

His people throughout the world were afraid of this madness that had come upon him; and they humbly knelt before him and worshipped him and called him their creator, as he had bidden them. But, out of his sight and his hearing, men whispered together and shook their heads over his folly; and, one by one, those who could do so, left his service and hid themselves in distant places where they hoped he might not reach them and punish their desertion.

2: Zohāk the Monster

AMONG the lesser rulers who paid tribute to Jemshid and acknowledged him their lord, there was a certain Arabian king named Merdās. This Merdās had a son, Zohāk, strong and bold and a fine horseman, more often in the saddle than not. It was this youth, much loved by his father, whom Ahrimān chose out to fulfil his evil designs against mankind. He sent the demon Eblis, in the shape of a traveller, a stranger to the Arab lands, to seek out Zohāk. When Eblis told Zohāk that he had journeyed many miles solely to see the brave and noble son of Merdās, a famed youth of whom he had heard much good, Zohāk, who had never before met with a flatterer, believed him and was glad to think that men who lived half the world away knew of him and respected his name.

The cunning Eblis soon won Zohāk's confidence and admiration, and when he said to him, 'I have a thing to tell you which is for no ears but yours alone,' Zohāk listened eagerly. 'You must first give me your word to speak of it to no one else and to obey me in whatever I demand of you,' warned Eblis then; and Zohāk, trusting him, asked no questions before swearing to be silent and to be obedient in all that Eblis might require of him.

'Then,' said Eblis, 'hear what I have to tell you. Your father Merdās is growing old, but you are young. It would be more fitting that you should reign in his place. You are a fine man, it is your right to rule. Slay your father and take his lands for your own.'

'I could not slay my own father,' exclaimed Zohāk. 'He loves me and he is a good man who has ever been kind to me.'

'Have faith in me,' said Eblis, 'and you will not only rule your father's lands, but, in time and by my help, the whole world will be yours.'

Zohāk was greatly tempted, yet still he said, 'I cannot kill my father. Tell me some other way to achieve what you have offered me.'

'There is no other way,' Eblis replied. Then his voice became for a moment no longer the voice of a flatterer or a tempter, but the voice of a merciless master. 'Do not forget, Zohāk, that you have sworn to obey me in whatever I shall demand of you.'

Won over by the promises of Eblis and greatly fearing his wrath, finally Zohāk yielded and bowed his head before the demon. 'Only tell me what I must do, and I will do it,' he said; and he heard in silence all that Eblis counselled.

Now, it was the custom of Merdās, each evening, to walk alone in his garden in quiet contemplation, forgetting the cares of sovereignty for an hour or so. The servants who attended him always waited at a distance, that they might not disturb his meditations, and they carried no lanterns, for Merdās loved the restful twilight and the dusk which followed it, with the faint, pale shapes of the flowers and their refreshing scents in the cool evening air. He ever walked along the same pathway, between the flowers, and he knew the way so well that he had no need to see it. Across that pathway Eblis now caused a deep pit to appear, and this pit he covered with straw. That same evening, as Merdās made his way along the path, never dreaming that his end was so near, he stepped upon the straw and fell into the pit. At his cry, his servants ran forward; but by the time that lights and ropes and ladders had been fetched, Merdās was dead and Zohāk was ruler of the Arab lands.

'Are you not well pleased with what I have performed for you?' Eblis asked him later.

'I am indeed well pleased,' Zohāk replied; and in truth, he was very well satisfied and no longer regretted that his father had had to die for him to achieve a throne.

'Have patience for only a little time, and you will be king of all the world,' promised Eblis, and he departed from the land, leaving Zohāk to rule how he would.

After a while had passed, Eblis returned to Arabia in the shape of a young man of open countenance, smiling and glib of tongue. He sought audience of Zohāk, saying, 'Lord, I am a skilled cook and I would take service with you. I can prepare many strange and delicate dishes, such as you have never before tasted, and you will not regret it if you find me a place in your royal kitchens.'

Zohāk did not send him away, and Eblis was true to his word. So appetizing were the dishes he prepared and so smooth were his speeches, that before many days had passed Zohāk had given him charge of the royal kitchens and set him over all the other cooks and scullions, with leave to do as he pleased.

Now, in those days men ate only the growing plants, the fruits and herbs and roots and crops which Ormuzd had provided for their sustenance. Their flocks and herds gave them wool and milk alone, and they ate no meat until Ahrimān, through Eblis, taught them to slaughter the four-footed beasts and the birds of the air and to eat their flesh.

As soon as he had charge of Zohāk's kitchens and the keys of Zohāk's storehouses were in his hands, Eblis began to fulfil Ahrimān's evil intentions. First he cooked an egg for Zohāk, who found it to his liking and demanded that Eblis should prepare a dish of eggs each day for him. This for a time Eblis did, flavouring the eggs cunningly with herbs and spices until Zohāk would no longer eat of any meal that was not made of eggs. And then one evening when Zohāk had praised him for the meal he had just set before him, Eblis said, 'Lord, you have not yet begun to taste of the delicacies which I can offer you. Have I your leave to prepare for your delight a new and tastier dish tomorrow?'

'It would be hard indeed for any man to prepare a tastier dish than you have cooked for me this evening,' said Zohāk, licking his lips over the meal he had just finished. 'Yet if it can be done, it is surely you who can do it.' And that night he hardly slept at all, so busy was his mind with wondering about the dish his clever cook would offer him the next day.

In the morning Eblis prepared a dish of quails and pheasant. When Zohāk saw and smelt it, his mouth watered, and eagerly and greedily he began to eat. When every mouthful was gone and the platters were empty, he said, 'Surely there can be no better food than this in all the world.'

'Nay, lord,' said Eblis, 'that is not so. Tomorrow's dish will be even better.'

The next day he brought to Zohāk a dish of lamb and chicken, crisp-roasted and flavoured with herbs. When every last morsel was eaten, Zohāk said, 'Not even you could surpass the meal you have set before me today, my friend.'

Eblis laughed. 'Tomorrow's meal will surpass today's as much as today's has outdone yesterday's,' he promised; and Zohāk could hardly wait for the morrow.

Again Eblis had not lied. The next day he set before Zohāk a dish of veal spiced skilfully and cooked in wine, and he stood by watching with a little scornful smile while Zohāk guzzled and gobbled it down and licked the platter clean.

Zohāk heaved a great sigh of regret that the meal was finished and the good food not there to be eaten all over again, and he said to Eblis, 'Surely no man, since the beginning of the world, has had such a servant as you. Ask any reward of me and it shall be yours.'

'It is reward enough for me to be permitted to serve you and to know that I have pleased you, lord. Yet there is one thing which I would ask of you, though I am unworthy that you should grant it.'

'What thing is that?' asked Zohāk.

'That you will allow me, lowly born as I am, to kiss your shoulders.'

'You may do so,' said Zohāk, 'and may such a favour raise you above other men.'

And so, as though he were Zohāk's equal and not the lowly cook he feigned to be, or as though he were Zohāk's own kinsman or close friend, Eblis stepped forward and, moving aside the king's royal robes, he kissed him on each shoulder. Then, in an instant, he had vanished, and Zohāk was alone. The young man had barely recovered his wits after the astonishment of seeing his cook disappear from sight as though he had been a spirit of the air—or, indeed, as though he had been the evil demon that he was—when he became aware of an unaccustomed sensation on his shoulders. He looked, and there, on either shoulder, where the demon's lips had touched his skin, the heads of two black serpents were appearing. Zohāk watched, appalled, as the serpents grew larger and larger until each was the size a large snake would have been if its tail and half its length had been hidden within the flesh and bones of his shoulder. Then, at last, the black bodies ceased to grow and remained swaying gently from side to side, hissing and darting forked tongues in and out.

Zohāk seized hold of one and tried to tear it from him, but to no avail. He cried aloud for help and his men came running; but they could not offer him the help he needed, though they tried in every way they might to cause the serpents to disappear; even, in desperation, cutting them from his shoulders. But as fast as they were hacked off, new black heads appeared again, and new black bodies grew long and strong.

And so it went for days and weeks, during which Zohāk had summoned to him every physician and scholar in the Arab lands, promising great rewards for any man who could find a way to rid him of the serpents. But all in vain; until one day when Eblis came again, this time in the shape of an old and learned physician, who said to him with grave authority, 'There is, lord, no way by which you may be rid of these serpents, for it is ordained that they shall be with you for as long as you live. Therefore seek no further to be

free of them. Instead, feed them with the nourishment they crave, and so keep them content and peaceable, and no harm will come to you from them. Indeed, in time they may well be sated with the food and grow weary of life and so fall first into sleep and then into death—who knows?' So spoke cunning Eblis, and Zohāk believed him, though he lied.

'What food must I give them?' Zohāk asked eagerly.

'The brains of two strong men each day,' replied Eblis; for it was the will of Ahrimān that in this manner there might be two men less in the world each day, for so long as the serpents endured.

'It shall be done,' said Zohāk; and Eblis left him, Ahrimān's evil work well begun.

From then on, with each day that passed, as the black serpents grew stronger, nourished by their ghastly food, so Zohāk grew ever more hardened, becoming more cruel and more ambitious, as the time drew nearer that Eblis had promised him, when he should rule the world. And Ahrimān, father of all evil, rejoiced, well pleased; for through Eblis and Zohāk he had taught men to kill like savage beasts for their food; and from an Arab princeling he had made a monster to plague mankind.

While Zohāk, as ruler of the Arab lands, grew daily more wicked, so did his overlord Jemshid grow more arrogant, vain, and overbearing; until not only some, but almost all, his lords and subject-kings could no longer bear his oppressions and they withdrew their allegiance from him and sought for someone among themselves who was brave and strong enough to be their leader and unite them in rebellion against Jemshid. And, monster though he was rumoured to be, one by one they looked to Zohāk for leadership, for he was said, also, to be fearless and strong as a giant. And so, thereby fulfilling Ahrimān's designs, they chose Zohāk to lead them against Jemshid, never dreaming that in Zohāk they were taking upon themselves a master far more merciless than the foolish, vain Jemshid.

When the time seemed favourable, Zohāk set himself at the head of a great army of subject-kings and princes, all bent on overthrowing Jemshid. Jemshid, with few left loyal to him, realized and regretted his folly too late. He surrendered his crown and his throne to Zohāk, seeking thereby to save his life; but Zohāk put him to a cruel death, sawing his body in two; and so ended the reign of poor, foolish Jemshid, who had once been so great a benefactor to mankind.

With one accord the kings and princes proclaimed their leader Zohāk to be Great King, and King of Kings, and lord of all the world. Rejoicing in his evil heart, Zohāk sat upon Jemshid's ivory throne, with Jemshid's turquoise crown upon his head. He took all Jemshid's treasure and riches for his own, and he forced Jemshid's two lovely young daughters, Shahrināz and Arnevāz, to be his unwilling wives.

With each day that passed Zohāk grew more powerful and more

cruel; and soon those who had helped to raise him up now longed to cast him down, yet dared not defy him. And, too, with each day that passed, two young men, of noble or of lowly birth, were seized and taken from their homes to Zohāk's palace, there to be slain, that their brains might be fed to Zohāk's black serpents.

3: Zohāk and Feridun

So time stretched on until one night when, as Zohāk lay asleep, he had a dream which filled him with terror. In this dream he saw himself dragged down from his throne and slain by a youth named Feridun. When he awoke, trembling, he sent his men to search everywhere throughout the world for a man or a boy or a babe whose name was Feridun, that he might destroy him and so escape the fate which had fallen upon him in his dream.

Now, there was a certain lord named Abtin, a kinsman of Jemshid, and he and his wife Firānek had three sons, the youngest of whom they called Feridun. As they searched about the world at their master's bidding, Zohāk's men learnt of this and made their way to Abtin's home to seize the child; but Abtin resisted them and was able to deny them entrance long enough for Firānek to flee to safety in the mountains with her children. Abtin was taken, in chains, to Zohāk, who put him to death and sent men out again to search every corner of the world for Abtin's youngest son; but in vain, for Firānek was safe with Feridun in a secret hiding-place, deep in the mountains.

The months and the years went by, while Feridun grew to manhood, longing for the time when he might avenge his father; and with each month and each year Zohāk became ever more fearful, expecting that at any hour the young hero of his nightmare might appear, to fall upon him and slay him; until he could think of little else all his waking hours, and in his sleep also, save Feridun. He sought to gather together a huge army of men and spirits and demons, that, when Feridun came, the young man might find his quarry well protected.

One morning Zohāk, now bent with dread and for ever glancing fearfully over his serpent-sprouting shoulders, was seated on his ivory throne in the hall of audience in his palace in his favourite city, Jerusalem. He was attended by his lords and his chief warriors; and while he was setting before them a proclamation and an oath to which he was demanding that each of his subjects should swear and set his name, a craftsman named Kāva, a master-smith, came to the palace seeking justice and was immediately brought before Zohāk.

'Who is this man?' Zohāk asked.

'Great King, I am Kāva the smith, and I seek justice.'

Zohāk, ever anxious—now, when it was too late—to win men's hearts, bade him, 'Speak that your king may give you justice.'

'Great King,' said Kāva, 'since you bid me speak, this is my complaint: once I had eighteen fine sons and now, of all these, only one remains alive. The others have been taken and unjustly slain. And today this last child of mine has been taken from my side and I fear for his life, also. Great King, save the life of my last son.'

'It is indeed a sorry tale you have to tell,' said Zohāk. 'Who is it that has dealt so ill with you and slain your sons? And for what cause?'

'Great King, forgive me, but it is you who have taken my elder sons, one after the other; and you now demand my youngest. Great King, I beg of you, spare me my last remaining son to bring me comfort in my old age, for I have never wronged you in any way, nor have I denied you my seventeen sons to feed the black serpents you nourish.'

Hastily Zohāk praised Kāva for his past loyalty and ordered that the smith's youngest son was to be spared and restored to him; and Kāva bowed before him in joy and thankfulness. Zohāk, pleased to have gained Kāva's gratitude, then sought to win his loyalty and bind him to his service. He commanded that the proclamation and the oath should be read to him, that Kāva might swear to serve his king, as had all the others present there that day. But when Kāva heard the oath in which those who swore to it declared their loyalty to Zohāk and maintained that he had ever been a just and merciful ruler and worthy of their loyalty and love, his honest heart rebelled, and he could not bring himself to swear to such a lie. He snatched the tablet on which the proclamation was engraved and flung it to the ground so that it was shattered, setting his foot upon it and crying out, 'Are all the men here cowards, that they are so swift to swear themselves slaves to one who is a slave of Ahrimān? And are they wanting in their wits, that they pronounce him good and just? Or is it that they are all as evil as he is? Never will I swear to such a lie or declare myself loyal to a servant of Ahrimān.' Then, while everyone, speechless, stared at him—Zohāk from anger and all the others in a kind of fearful admiration—Kāva strode from the hall of audience, hurrying his terrified son before him.

While all those in Zohāk's palace fearfully made haste to protest themselves faithful to him, Kāva went home, and taking his smith's leathern apron, he fastened it to the head of a spear; then, carrying this spear and apron like a banner, he made his way to the marketplace and there he spoke to the people, bidding them rise against the monster who ruled the world, and urging them to go with him to Feridun and ask his leadership; for Kāva had long known that secret which Zohāk would have given his most prized possessions to know—the hiding-place of the young kinsman of Jemshid. The people, who had for so long endured without hope, now flocked to Kāva from every street and from every corner of the city; and it was a large and eager crowd of men, young and old, rich and poor, carrying with them any weapons they could find, who followed Kāva's apron on the spear, which he held aloft as he led them from Jerusalem in search of Feridun. As they went, from every village they passed and from every place where men had their dwellings, others joined with them, shouting out their hatred and defiance of Zohāk, and calling upon Ormuzd to be with them and help them to destroy the evil works of the wicked followers of Ahrimān, and to restore justice and liberty to the world once more.

When the sentinels who guarded Feridun's secret fortress saw the crowd which marched towards them, they ran swiftly to Feridun with their tidings, and joyfully he and those men whom he had been gathering around him through the past years, rode out to greet the newcomers. Speedily then, over the next few days, Feridun made ready for immediate war, though the numbers of his warriors were but a tenth of those Zohāk could muster. On an appointed day Feridun rode with his small army towards the River Tigris, to free the world from the yoke of Ahrimān and his servant Zohāk; and before this army, beside young Feridun, rode Kāva, once again bearing aloft his leathern apron—but now it was set upon brocade and sewn with gems, and decorated with ribands of crimson, violet, and gold, which fluttered from it in the breeze. And to all who followed it, both on that great day and for many, many generations to come, the Banner of Kāva was a holy standard, a revered inspiration; and the raising of the Banner of Kāva was ever a call to arms and a rallying point for all valiant men.

When they came to the River Tigris, Feridun sent for the captain who had charge of those who guarded the crossing of the river, and he demanded that he should make ready his boats to ferry the army over. But the man replied, 'I have my orders from Zohāk, Great King, and King of Kings, and from no man else. No one may cross the river unless he can show me a pass stamped with the seal of Zohāk the king.'

'I need no consent of Zohāk the monster before I can cross this river,' exclaimed Feridun; and crying out to the others to follow him, he rode his horse into the water and the brave beast swam across. Close after Feridun came Kāva with the Banner; and behind these two came their followers, all shouting out their defiance of Zohāk and their contempt for his passes and seals. On the farther bank Feridun paused until all had safely crossed, then speedily he led them on. In the same manner they crossed the River Euphrates and went on towards Jerusalem.

A league from the city, Feridun reined in his horse and paused, watching the sunlight turning to gold the tall towers and flat roofs of Jerusalem. 'It seems strange to me,' he said, 'that so fair a place should be the den of so foul a monster.' Then he frowned a little. 'It will be a city well guarded and we shall be far outnumbered. Our hope is in the speed of our attack alone.' Bidding the others follow him as fast as they might, he spurred his horse into a gallop; and so, with the Banner of Kāva streaming on before them, Feridun's little army came against Zohāk's favourite city.

Now, it happened that at this time Zohāk was no longer in Jerusalem. He had left the city almost immediately after Kāva's defiance of him, for a town some miles away, to take oaths of loyalty and to win military support from those who dwelt there. So swift was Feridun's progress that he was at the very gate of Jerusalem before word of his coming could be sent to Zohāk. Although Feridun had expected to enter the city with difficulty, and only after hard fighting, to his great joy he entered as easily as though he were a merchant leading a string of pack-horses laden with tempting wares, rather than a warrior at the head of an army. For those who guarded the gate and the walls fled when they saw him coming, and the townsfolk flung open the gate, crying to him as their deliverer and welcoming back their kinsfolk and neighbours who had left them to follow Kāva. Through the streets and on to the palace, to the cheers of the people, rode Feridun; but at the palace Zohāk's hideous demon guards, terrifying to see and all well armed, stood against him. Calling encouragement to his followers and swinging to the left and right of him with a heavy bull-headed mace, Feridun rode through the palace doors, demons with cracked skulls falling either side of him, and Zohāk's servants fleeing before him like timid deer before a hungry lion. In the very throne-room of Zohāk he leapt from his horse and, ascending the dais, he seated himself upon Jemshid's ivory throne and set Jemshid's turquoise crown upon his head.

Whenever Zohāk was absent from Jerusalem it was his custom to give charge of the palace to his chamberlain, no demon, but a man of great dignity who did not take his office lightly, and who ever moved about the palace with more pomp, and spoke with more deliberation, than any king on earth; for which reason he had long been nicknamed Slow-and-Staid. When someone now came to him with the news that a strange young man, at the head of a small army, had entered the palace and was sitting upon the throne, Slow-and-Staid was filled with consternation; and had they not been too distraught and too afraid themselves, Zohāk's servants would have delighted in the unimaginable sight of Slow-and-Staid running like a madman from his quarters to the throne-room, to see for himself how matters stood. When he was aware that all the demon guards were dead and all Zohāk's masterless servants of no more use than a crowd of frightened children; and when he found armed strangers everywhere and an unknown young warrior seated upon the throne, he knew immediately that open loyalty to Zohāk would be profitless to one who wished to remain in his high office no matter who ruled the world. He paused to get his breath and set straight his disordered garments, then, a stately figure, with his customary grave dignity he approached the throne and bowed low before Feridun. 'Greetings, young stranger,' he said. 'I am the chamberlain of this palace and I bid you welcome in the name of all Jerusalem. Give me your orders and I shall see to it that you are obeyed.'

Feridun commanded wine to be brought and a feast to be prepared and musicians—with their arched-harps, their flutes, and their box-lyres which were adorned with carven bulls—to play for him, that he might fittingly celebrate the capture of the palace and the freeing of Jerusalem from the monster Zohāk; and Slow-and-Staid saw that all was done as Feridun desired.

In the palace there were two whose joy at the coming of Feridun was as great, and greater, than any man's. Shahrināz and Arnevāz, the daughters of Jemshid, were happy, as they had never thought to be happy again. Feridun went to the women's quarters to seek them out, that he might himself tell them they were free to go or to remain in the palace in all honour, as they wished. They were both still lovely and not yet old, and they chose to remain in the palace, as the respected and beloved wives of Feridun.

The feasting and the rejoicing in the palace lasted for several days; and while it was yet at its height, Slow-and-Staid slipped quietly away and rode off to his master Zohāk to report to him all that had happened. When Zohāk heard that Kāva the smith had returned to Jerusalem at the head of an army, beside a beautiful young stranger, he grew pale, remembering the young stranger of his nightmare, whose name was Feridun.

'His body is as slim and straight as a cypress tree, and his face as fair as the silver moon in its topmost branches,' said the chamberlain. 'He rode into your palace on horseback and he slew all your demon guards.'

Zohāk would not let himself even think of that Feridun who was to be his downfall. 'Young men are rash and impetuous,' he said. 'They act before they think.' With an effort he sought to make light of the matter, so as to soothe his own fears. 'If he comes as a guest, he must be humoured. A worthy host allows much liberty to his guests.'

'Great King,' said Slow-and-Staid, 'he sits on your throne with your crown on his head and he orders your servants as though they were his own.'

'An arrogant guest is a trial, but no disaster,' said Zohāk desperately. 'A good host will, in courtesy, overlook the failings of his guests.'

'Great King,' said the chamberlain, 'if he is your guest, why is it that he goes into your women's quarters, where no guest should dare to venture, and from among your wives seeks out the daughters of Jemshid and speaks lovingly to them?'

At that Zohāk could no longer contain his anger. His eyes blazing, he leapt to his feet, calling his chamberlain traitor and false servant, that he had allowed a stranger to lord it in his palace. 'Never again,' he cried furiously, 'shall I give into your hands the charge of my palace and possessions. You are unworthy of so great an honour.'

'It is unlikely, Great King,' said Slow-and-Staid dryly, 'that you will ever again give the charge of your palace to me or to any other man.' And he left Zohāk and rode back to Jerusalem.

Zohāk called for his bodyguard of demons and for a fast horse; then, wearing his iron armour which no weapon could pierce, he rode at a wild gallop to Jerusalem. There, leaving his bodyguard to storm the city gate, now held by Feridun's men, he quickly made his way into the city and the palace by a narrow, secret path. By means of a noosed rope, skilfully cast upwards to catch upon a pinnacle, he climbed to the tallest tower of the palace, from where he could

look down into all the courts and gardens spread below him. Among fair flowers and fountains he saw Shahrināz with Feridun, who had not yet been told of the attack upon the city gate. In jealous fury, all caution forgotten, Zohāk drew a dagger, and flinging down the rope's end into the garden where Feridun sat at ease, and shouting out curses upon the heads of the young stranger and his own faithless wife, he slipped down the length of the rope with the speed of a lightning flash and flung himself upon Feridun like a death-bearing storm-wind.

But Feridun was as swift as his attacker. He snatched up his bull-headed mace and with it struck Zohāk such a blow upon his iron helmet that he was thrown to the ground and lay there stunned and senseless. Feridun would then have cut off his head without a moment's thought, and so rid the world of the monster who had ruled it for too long, but that, at the moment when he raised his sword, Ormuzd sent a spirit to him, a wondrous being in a cloud of shining light, who bade him spare Zohāk's life.

'Bear him instead,' said this good spirit, 'to the mountains, and there, locked in their deepest heart, leave him for ever, as a warning to all future men.'

Feridun obeyed the command of Ormuzd and bound Zohāk with ropes of plaited lion-skin, so strong that, even with all his evil strength strained to the utmost, he could never break free of them. Then Feridun had him borne to Mount Demāvend, the highest peak of the Elburz Mountains, and left there, deep inside the mountain, chained and powerless and with his two black serpents, a miserable prisoner and a warning to all mankind, that those who serve Ahrimān too well must one day answer for it.

To the great joy of the many who had for so long suffered his tyrannies, Feridun caused Zohāk's name to be erased from every spot where it was written, and his own set in its place; all Zohāk's cruel laws he repealed, smashing to dust the tablets on which they were engraved; and he bade every man live in peace and work in freedom for the good of all mankind and for his own happiness. And so, with Feridun as Great King, and King of Kings, and ruler of all the world, and with the subject-kings of every land bowing in homage before him, willingly and gladly, peace and happiness came to all men for a time; the goodness of Ormuzd was everywhere and the evil of Ahrimān was stilled and silent.

4: The Sons of Feridun

THREE sons were born to Feridun. Shahrināz was the mother of the two elder boys, while the third and youngest was the child of Arnevāz. They grew to strong, bold young men, and Feridun sent one of his most trusted counsellors to search through all the world for wives for them. This wise man at last found three sisters, daughters of King Sarv of South Western Arabia, who in every way seemed fitted to be the brides of the three sons of the lord of all the world. Feridun approved his counsellor's choice, and the three young men set out for Arabia to marry and bring home the three princesses.

Now, Feridun was then just fifty years old, he had reigned for many years and he believed that the time had come when he should rest from the toil of government and hand over the rule of the world to younger men. And moreover, it seemed good to him to choose his successors while he himself still lived, and therefore might offer to the younger kings the benefits of the wisdom and the knowledge which his years of experience had brought him. He loved his sons equally, and so he determined to divide the world among them—a decision which was to bring much pain and grief to men for generation upon generation to come. Yet, though he did not find it hard to divide the world into three great empires, since these three empires were not, and could not be, of equal size and importance, he was unable to make up his mind as to which of his sons he would allot each region. So he decided to test each one to discover, if he could, which of them would make the best and wisest ruler, that he might give to him the rule of the middlemost lands of the world, which formed the most important and the largest of the three empires.

Accordingly, on receiving word that the three young men, each with his bride, had started on their homeward journey from South Western Arabia, he set out secretly from Ecbatana, his capital, to meet them on the way. At a certain place along the road which they would take, by the grace and with the help of Ormuzd, he transformed himself into a dragon, fire-breathing and fearful to behold, and waited for the travellers to approach.

First came the cavalcade of Salm, his eldest son, with Salm himself riding a little way ahead. When the prince reached the place where

his father was hidden, Feridun, in his dragon shape, stepped in the young man's path, roaring and breathing forth flames, and stamping with immense clawed feet, until the ground trembled.

Immediately he saw the dragon, Salm reined in his horse. 'A man of sense does not attempt the impossible. Only a fool would attack and provoke a dragon,' he said; and turning his horse, he galloped back to his followers and led them home by another way.

Feridun, well pleased at the prudence which Salm had shown, concealed himself again, and when Tur, his second son, approached, he put himself in his path, as he had done with Salm. As soon as Tur saw the dragon he set an arrow to his bow, spurred on his horse and charged the fearful monster, crying out, 'If a man be threatened, what matter if it be by a single warrior or by a monster huge as a hill? A brave man refuses no challenge.'

Feridun made haste to hide himself, and he watched while Tur, glancing keenly to all sides, the arrow still ready in his bow, led his retinue safely past the spot where the dragon had stood to threaten him. Then, approving Tur's courage, Feridun awaited the coming of his third son.

As Iraj, the youngest son, approached, Feridun, still in dragon shape and as he had done with his two elder sons, stepped into the young man's path. Iraj reined in his horse immediately, but neither fled nor charged. Instead he raised his head high and called out at the top of his voice, 'Away with you, creature! How do you, you who are no more than a little kitten, dare venture on the path where lions go? I am the son of a brave warrior, and my two brothers are not far away. We three together are a match, and more than a match, for any enemy in all the world. For are we not, all three, the sons of mighty Feridun? If you had ever before heard the name and the deeds of Feridun, ugly monster, you would not be waiting here for his sons. Now begone, before I smash your skull for you.'

Best pleased of all with the conduct of Iraj, who had shown not only prudence and courage, but had also made plain his admiration and respect for his father and his love for his brothers and the trust and confidence he had in them, Feridun made off hastily. Back in his palace, and in his own shape once again, he awaited his three sons at the gate, welcoming each with joy and telling him of how, in dragon form, he had tested him, and found them, all three, to be sons such as any father might take pride in.

Then, according to their merits, he divided the world among them. To Salm, the eldest, he gave the western parts, Greece, and Rome and all kingdoms which made up the Lands of the West. To Tur, the second son, he gave the eastern lands, Turkey, and China and all the other regions lying beyond the River Oxus, which made up the Lands of the East, and which took from him their name, coming to be known as the empire of Turān. And to Iraj, the youngest son, he gave all the lands which lay in the middle of the world, around the Tigris and Euphrates rivers, together with Egypt and the Arab kingdoms and the northern realms of the Scythians; and from his name they came to be called Iran, or, sometime, Persia. And to Iraj, also, Feridun handed his seal and his royal ring, and upon his head he set not only the ancient turquoise crown of Jemshid, but also the new, glittering tiara which had been made for Feridun himself, the tall golden crown of the Great King, and King of Kings. And he led Iraj, not to Jemshid's ivory throne, but to the magnificent golden throne which he had caused to be made for him, early in his reign, as ruler of the world, and upon this throne he seated Iraj. And so, to his youngest son he gave the greatest honours of all, because he considered him the most worthy.

Thus, from love of his three sons, Feridun divided the world among them, and never, since that day, has the world been wholly at peace but, in one corner or another, in this land or in that, there has been strife and war.

At first, for a short time, in the faraway Lands of the West, and in nearer Turān, all appeared well enough; while Persia prospered, ruled by young Iraj, who was ever counselled and encouraged by his father. But beneath their calm and their smiles and their apparent content, envy and covetousness grew in the hearts of the two elder brothers. Salm, in the Lands of the West, grew daily more ambitious and more discontented. 'I am the eldest son,' he thought. 'It is I who should have been Great King, and King of Kings.' He wrote a letter to Tur, sounding out his brother's heart, and he sent it to him by a messenger mounted on a swift camel. When Tur read this letter, his own spite and envy, which needed little rousing, were stirred by it, and he too thought, 'Iraj is the youngest of us three, why should the most prized crown of all be his? Our father should have divided the middle lands between Salm and me.' And he sent word back to his brother that they should meet together secretly to talk of their grievances and the injustice which had been done to them.

They met; and the words of each but served to inflame and increase the rancour of the other. 'Our father has wronged us,' they said, in their anger talking folly. 'We, his elder sons, have been given empires on the fringes of the world, far from our father's love and friendship. Exiled, we languish, while Iraj, the youngest of us, lords it as Great King, and takes all our father's love and all the honours which should be ours. It is Iraj who should be banished from our father's sight and sent far away to a little kingdom on the edge of the world, while you and I, my brother, divide his empire between us and add it to the lands which we possess already.'

So much in agreement they were, that they sent a letter to their father, blaming him for the manner in which he had dealt with them, and setting forth their demands.

Feridun was greatly saddened by the greed of his two elder sons, and angered by their disrespect. He wrote in reply to them, chiding them for their ambition; and he told Iraj of their jealousy, urging him to have a care of them for the future. But Iraj could not believe that his brothers wished him harm; and though he answered his father with courtesy and respect, as a good son should, he believed him mistaken in his judgement.

When Salm and Tur received Feridun's reply, they said bitterly, 'If we may not rule Persia, then neither shall Iraj. If our father will not withdraw his favour from our younger brother, then Iraj must die.' And they discussed how it might be brought about.

But it was Iraj himself who made it easy for them to commit the crime they planned. The more he thought on his father's warning, the more he was saddened by what he believed to be a misunderstanding, an old man's error of judgement. 'It is not right that there should be ill feeling between the sons of the same father,' he said to Feridun. 'I shall go to my brothers, that the three of us together, remembering the great love there was between us when we were boys, may discuss and resolve the differences which now separate us. And so I shall put an end to your doubts of their friendship, and prove your suspicions of them to be without cause.'

In vain Feridun repeated his warnings. Iraj, having neither guile nor hatred for any man in his own heart, could not believe these emotions to have a home in the hearts of his brothers. He sent to Salm and Tur, arranging a time and a place for a meeting. Salm and Tur could hardly believe their good fortune, that Iraj was thus putting himself into their power. They received him with all courtesy and in seeming friendliness; and they ordered that, with much ceremony, the men of their two armies should be drawn up in their ranks to welcome him. But when they saw how both the warriors of the Lands of the West and the men of Turān smiled at his coming and, unbidden, raised their cheers to the very clouds in greeting, any last doubts they may have felt about their intended course vanished at the sound. 'He is too well loved by far,' they said. 'He is a danger to us and he must die.'

The three brothers entered the splendid pavilion which had been set up for their meeting, and seating themselves they discussed the matters which troubled them. When Salm and Tur had made their complaints to him, Iraj said, 'Willingly shall I give up to you the imperial tiara and the golden throne of the King of Kings, my brothers. For I would rather have your love and goodwill than all the treasure of Persia and all the imperial army. I do not even ask of you in return a portion of the Lands of the West or of Turān. I would be content with your affection, even though you sent me into exile in the farthest corner of the world.'

Though once their brother's offer might have contented them, it was no longer so. The cheers of their warriors, when Iraj had appeared before them, still echoed in their envious hearts. Tur rose and asked angrily, 'Why should we trust you, Salm and I? You will cheat us and turn our own people against us. And besides, our father loves you too well to permit us to accept the offer you make to us. No, there can be no justice for us while you live.' And raising up the heavy gilded throne upon which he had been seated, he brought it down with all his might upon thc head of Iraj and felled him to the ground.

'Good brothers, do not kill me,' pleaded Iraj. 'I swear to you that all I have shall be yours. Leave me my life and I will hide myself far away where I shall be forgotten. No one shall ever hear my name again, or speak of me. I swear it to you.'

They heard him unmoved. Tur drew his dagger and with it struck Iraj again and again, until he was dead.

When he learnt what had befallen at the meeting of his three sons, Feridun's heart was filled with sorrow and rage: sorrow for Iraj and rage against his elder brothers. With the death of Iraj, Feridun had lost not one, but all of his three sons, for Iraj was murdered and Feridun was ncver to forgive Tur and Salm for that murder as long as he lived. He grieved, too, that neither the Arabian princess who had been his queen, nor any of his other wives, had given Iraj a son to avenge and succeed him. Sadly Feridun took back the tall tiara of the Great King, and King of Kings, and seated himself once more upon the golden throne and took again upon his ageing shoulders the government of Persia.

Then one day it came to his ears that in the women's quarters of the apartments of Iraj, there was a certain serving-girl whom Iraj had greatly loved, and who was soon to bear her master's child. Feridun sent for this girl and promised her, 'Your son shall be his father's heir and rule the empire of Persia.'

But when the child was born, it was a daughter, and Feridun wept bitter tears. Then, after a time, he thought, 'I am not yet so old that I may not live to see a great-grandson of mine avenge Iraj.' And he took the babe into his care and brought her up with all kindness, and betrothed her to a descendant of Jemshid. When the day for her marriage came, she was wedded with ceremony fitting for the daughter of a Great King.

In due time a son was born to her, whom his parents named Minucher. Feridun, rejoicing, at once sent for the child and saw that he was, from his earliest years, brought up as befitted a warrior. By all the best instructors in Persia, he had him taught fighting skill and battle-craft, all feats of arms, and horsemanship. And as soon as Minucher was of an age to understand what would one day be required of him, Feridun saw to it that the boy knew that his one purpose in life must be the downfall and death of his great-uncles, Salm and Tur; and that the only ambition he was allowed was this revenge for his grandfather's murder.

Feridun watched Minucher's development jealously and eagerly, and marked with satisfaction how apt a pupil he was, and a fierce joy warmed a little his sad old heart and brought a promise of rest to his tormented mind, as his great-grandson grew up and the day of vengeance came nearer.

From the Lands of the West and from Turān, Salm and Tur, also, through their spies, watched the progress of Minucher from child to skilled warrior; and then, because he who is ready has ever the advantage, and he who attacks first has the battle half won, they called up their armies and the armies of their subject-kings. Then Salm, with those kings and princes of the West whose overlord he was, marched into Turān to join forces with his brother.

Feridun smiled grimly when the news was brought to him of how his two elder sons were about to invade Persia. 'We have long awaited them, and we are ready,' he said; and he placed the imperial army of Persia in the charge of young Minucher. 'My child,' he said to him, 'the time has come for which we have so long prepared, and the day of vengeance is very close. May great Ormuzd be with you; and when next we meet, may my beloved son Iraj have been avenged.'

The Banner of Kāva was raised high, the brazen battle-trumpets sounded and the warriors of the Great King and of his subject rulers went forth. The armies of Tur and Salm crossed the River Oxus into Persia and drew up in battle array. Soon the two armies faced each other across the plain.

Minucher had been trained to be more than merely a brave warrior. He had studied also the stratagems of war; and, moreover, he had learned the value of respect for those older warriors whose years had brought them the experience which, for all his studies, he still lacked. In charge of the left flank of his army he placed an old general, a warrior of note. To the right flank he assigned a younger, but much respected, leader, Sām, the ruler of the small kingdom of Zābulestān; and with Sām, another, older general. Minucher himself led the middle ranks where the Banner of Kāva streamed proudly in the breeze, and beside him was old Sarv, king of South Western Arabia, to aid him with good counsel.

The two armies stood awaiting the signal for attack: war-horses and chariots, elephants and warriors—the warriors well armed with their leathern helmets strengthened with iron and their short, fitted jackets plated with bronze—all of them poised to advance. In those final moments before battle was joined, Tur rode out before his men and called his defiance to Minucher. 'Tell young Minucher that I have no fear of him. And ask him what claim he has to a throne and a crown, grandson of a serving-girl that he is.'

When someone repeated these words to Minucher, he only laughed. 'Let the fool say what he will. All praise be to Ormuzd, Iraj was my grandfather, the Great King Feridun himself declares it, therefore who dare deny it?' And he gave orders for the attack.

Throughout the hard battle which followed, Minucher proved himself an able commander, as skilled in strategy as in combat. All his years of training had not been in vain. Under his command the warriors of Persia won a great victory; and it was by his hand that first Tur, and then Salm, were slain. Their defeated armies fled back across the River Oxus, the battle was over and Iraj avenged.

When word of victory was brought to Feridun, he rejoiced and gave thanks to Ormuzd. And when Minucher returned to him, he embraced the young man and praised him for a true grandson of Iraj; and he confirmed his wish that he should be his heir. With his favourite son avenged, Feridun no longer had reason for his grim grasp on life; and soon the old man died, at peace and content, and was succeeded, as he had wished, by Minucher.

5: Zāl the White-Haired

AMONG those who had fought the most valiantly for Minucher in his battle against his great-uncles, Salm and Tur, had been the renowned young warrior Sām, king of Zābulestān, a subject-monarch who paid tribute to the Great King. Sām had early won fame for himself as a fighting-man, and he was much respected as a brave and just ruler of his small country.

One day a son was born to Sām's fair young queen. The child's birth had been awaited eagerly, not only by his parents but by all in the palace; yet when the boy was born there was no one in the queen's apartments with the courage to go to Sām with word of those tidings which should have been so happy—yet were not. For the child was like no other child in all the world. He was fair and unblemished in form and feature, with well-made limbs which promised to grow as straight and strong as his father's, and he had his mother's fine dark eyes—but his hair was as white as the hair of an old man of four score years and more.

The queen wept bitterly at the sight of her strange child, and her women trembled; and for seven whole days no one dared to tell Sām that his son had been born. But at last his wife's old nurse, a woman of great courage, who loved her mistress dearly, said, 'We can hide this thing no longer. Ill would it be for us all if the king were to discover the truth for himself, and to learn, moreover, that we had concealed it from him for so long, as though it were indeed some shameful secret. Soon he will come to ask concerning you, dear queen. It were best we told him freely of how matters stand, before he comes to see for himself.'

This brave old woman went to Sām, her face all smiles and her voice ringing joyfully, as though she brought him only the best of tidings. Yet inwardly her heart beat fearfully, and she could hardly still the trembling of her limbs. 'Rejoice, lord king,' she said, 'for you have been much blessed by Ormuzd and you have a son. He is as fine and beautiful a babe as any father might wish for. From his lusty cries and sturdy limbs it is plain to all that he will be a strong man and a great warrior, a fitting son for any king.' Sām leapt to his feet, laughing aloud in his joy; and the nurse went on hastily, 'From the top of his head to the soles of his feet he is without blemish, lord king. In one respect only he differs from other children—as indeed the son of a king should differ from the sons of all lesser men. His limbs are ivory, his eyes are jet, and his little mouth is a red ruby. But his hair is priceless silver—as pale as moonlight, as white as the pure snow which crowns the mountain tops. Your son is indeed the fairest of all children, lord king, so rejoice and give thanks to Ormuzd.' At the frown that came to Sām's brow, and at the bewildered and unbelieving look that came to his eyes, her voice faltered and ceased.

'What are you saying to me, woman? That he has hair as white as snow? You jest with me. No new-born babe ever had snow-white hair.'

'It is true, lord king,' she whispered, terrified.

'Take me to him, that I may see this wonder for myself,' demanded Sām.

While the other women crowded together fearfully at the end of the queen's chamber, as far from him as they might, and the old nurse alone stood beside the weeping queen, Sām looked down at his sleeping son and saw that it was indeed as the old woman had told him: the babe's hair was white.

'You bid me give thanks to Ormuzd, woman,' he said at last. 'But this child is no gift from Ormuzd. Rather it is surely some frightful jest of Ahrimān sent to shame me before all men. From end to end of the empire of Persia men will talk of it and laugh, how the king of Zābulestān fathered a child that was old and hoary on the very day of its birth. And worse than that, who knows what monster of evil this creature may become in future years?' Then Sām prayed, 'Great Ormuzd, forgive me if, mistaken, I act wrongly or cruelly; for I act only as I believe I should, in thus ridding myself and my people of this spawn of Ahrimān.' And he ordered that the child was to be taken from the palace immediately and carried to the desert and there left to die. 'Thus may we be freed from this curse which Ahrimān has sent upon us,' he said; and then, as did his wife and all her women, he wept for grief.

And so, for fear that he would grow to be some evil creature, beloved of Ahrimān, who would work harm to men, Sām's little white-haired son was carried from the palace, out to the desert, and left lying at the foot of the Elburz Mountains.

The child lay on the hard, stony ground in the burning rays of the sun, and his crying grew feebler with each minute that passed. But before his cries ceased altogether, they came to the sharp ears of the magical Simurgh bird as she sought prey for her newly hatched

nestlings. Her keen eyes soon sighted him and, swooping low on immense widespread black wings, she snatched him up in her strong talons and carried him off to her eyrie on the very topmost peak of Mount Demāvend, the highest point of the Elburz Mountains, to be food for her young. But the hungry nestlings turned from the strange creature she had brought to them, and would not eat; and so she went in search of other prey. When she returned with a dead fawn, the child was huddled among the soft, downy bodies of her young, accepted by them as one of themselves. So the Simurgh, also, accepted Sām's son as her own, and fed him with the tenderest portions of deer's flesh; and as her fledglings grew and flourished, so did the child. In time he grew first to a lovely boy and then to a beautiful youth, tall and straight, with long white hair that reached to his waist. He ran and leapt on the mountains and about the foothills, and men passing across the desert on their way to the city of Zābul sometimes caught a glimpse of this strange, lovely creature and carried word of the wondrous sight with them to their destination. And so one day the tidings came to the ears of Sām and he suspected at once that his son was not dead, but that, in some unknown way, he had been preserved—perhaps by the will of Ormuzd—and at once he determined to go to the Elburz Mountains to see his son for himself.

With a few followers he rode into the desert, to the foot of Mount Demāvend. From there he could see, far above him on the topmost crag, the nest of the Simurgh, and beside it on the rocks, the huge bird herself and a slim youth whose hair was white. But though he tried in every way, accompanied or alone, to climb the mountain, he could in no manner reach the top. At last he gave up his vain attempts and, descending sadly, he prayed to Ormuzd. 'Great lord of the universe, if he whom I can see aloft is indeed the child whom I sent out to his death many years ago, and if he is truly my son and no evil monster sent by Ahrimān, then let me behold him close and speak with him.' Thus Sām prayed and waited for an answer to his prayer.

Away in her eyrie the Simurgh looked down with her keen eyes, and by her magical wisdom she knew who was the man whom she saw far below her. 'Down there,' she said to her foster-child, 'stands Sām, ruler of Zābulestān. He is your father and he it was who left you to die in the wilderness. He now repents of that deed and is come in search of you. He has a father's love, a kingdom and an honoured life among men to offer you. Willingly would I have you stay here with me for ever, for you are as dear to me as any of my brood. Yet you are a man and it is fitting that you should live the life of a man among other men. The time has come for you to leave me.' She took the youth gently in her talons and stretching wide her wings like a black cloud, she flew with him down to the foot of the mountain and set him before Sām.

Sām looked at his son and saw that he was fashioned like any other man—though more beautiful of face and form than most—save that his hair was snow-white. Yet that seemed now to be a mark of beauty and no blemish. Overjoyed, father and son embraced; then both offered their thanks to the Simurgh, who said to the youth, 'It is the time for us to part, yet today you are no less my child than you were upon that day when I first found you, weak and helpless, and in the years to come my love and my care will still be yours.' She plucked a feather from her wing and gave it to Sām's son, saying, 'If ever you have need of my help, burn this feather of mine and I will know of it and come to you, wherever you may be.' Once again she spread wide her wings, and like a black cloud was gone, back to her eyrie on the highest crag of Mount Demāvend.

Sām and his son went gladly home; and there, with great happiness and much ceremony, Sām named the youth Zāl and proclaimed him his heir.

That Zāl had been nurtured by a bird and had grown up far from the dwellings of men and that his hair was as white as snow, soon mattered as little to any in Zābulestān as it mattered to his father Sām. For Zāl quickly proved himself wise beyond his years, as great a warrior as Sām, and the best of horsemen; and he was soon loved by all in Zābulestān. To observe the ways of other men, he travelled much, not only about his father's small kingdom, but also in the other lands of Minucher's empire.

6: Zāl and Rudāba

ONE day, with his followers, Zāl passed through the land of Kābulestān, and finding it to his liking, he ordered his pavilions to be set up on the banks of a fair river, and gave it as his intention to remain in that place for a few days.

Now, Kābulestān was ruled by a certain King Mehrāb, who owed allegiance and paid tribute to the Great King. But Mehrāb was of the line of the Arabian Zohāk, who had been tempted and led astray by Eblis and had, by his wicked life, served Ahrimān so well; and Mehrāb had no love for Minucher, whose great-grandfather Feridun had broken Zohāk's power, and he took it very ill that he had to call Minucher his overlord. Mehrāb's kingdom was not large enough and his army was too small for him to rebel openly, but he soothed his resentful heart by plotting continually against Minucher, and cheating him of a portion of the tribute-money whenever it was possible. All this Minucher had known for several years, yet for the sake of Mehrāb's subjects, who would have suffered had Kābulestān been invaded, he chose to ignore it; and though he tolerated Mehrāb's disloyalty he showed him no favour; while all his faithful subject-kings, like Sām, had nothing but ill to say of Mehrāb, and would willingly have seen him punished. It was for this reason that Zāl, on deciding to remain in Kābulestān, chose to lodge in his pavilion rather than accept the hospitality which Mehrāb sent to offer him.

Zāl had intended to remain no more than a few days encamped beside the river, but someone, seeking to divert him, told him that the plotter Mehrāb had a daughter, Rudāba, renowned for her beauty, not only in her own land of Kābulestān, but throughout many kingdoms. 'She is brighter than the sun. Tall and straight she stands, like a plane tree. Her skin is as pale and smooth as ivory, and her long, long hair has the sheen of a raven's wing. Her eyes are narcissus flowers, and her brows are two black bows. Her lips are pomegranate blossoms, and her smile is paradise,' Zāl was told.

These words so impressed him that he remained in Kābulestān, encamped beside the river, for far longer than he had intended, in the hope—unlikely to be fulfilled—of catching a glimpse of Mehrāb's daughter.

On the opposite bank of the river lay the city of Kābul, with King

Mehrāb's palace, set around with fair gardens stretching down to the water's edge; and Zāl hoped that some day the Princess Rudāba might walk in those gardens. And so it went for a month or more.

Rudāba's serving-women who brought word to the women's quarters of all that passed outside the palace walls, told her of the young prince of Zābulestān who had set up his pavilions across the river, who had been reared by a bird and was said to be second to none in beauty, for all that his hair was white like the hair of an old man. Their words so caught the imagination of Rudāba that she asked her father, in as careless a manner as she could feign, whether it were true or not, that which her women had told her concerning Zāl.

'It is indeed true, my child,' answered Mehrāb. 'All men speak well of young Zāl. He is a fine warrior like his father Sām, and a generous prince, and as beautiful as any man could wish to be, in spite of his white hair. Indeed, many consider that the colour of his hair but serves to increase his beauty and leaves him with no equal in looks in all the world. This I can well believe, having seen him.'

Mehrāb's words of praise so stirred Rudāba that soon she could think of nothing else all day save the young prince of Zābulestān; and all night she dreamt of him, white-haired and as splendid in appearance as one of the good immortal spirits who served Ormuzd. And so it went for a month or more.

Among the women who served her, Rudāba had five Turanian slaves, girls as young as their mistress, pretty and high-spirited, whom she preferred above all her servants and who, for their part, were devoted to her. To these girls Rudāba confessed her secret, that she believed herself to have fallen in love with Zāl, though she had never even seen him.

The Turanian girls, though young, were not foolish, and they could see only unhappiness for their beloved mistress in this fancy of hers. Prudently they sought to change her mind for her. 'Dearest princess,' they pleaded, 'you have not seen him, so how can you love him? Besides, did he not discourteously refuse all your father's offers of friendship and hospitality, slighting the king and disdaining to be his guest? And has he not set up his pavilions over the river, remaining there, proud and haughty, despising the noble king of Kābulestān and ignoring his servants when they carry to him your father's hospitable messages, as though they were stones by the wayside rather than the trusted servants of a king? Besides, no other man since the beginning of time has been born old and hoary-haired. This Zāl is more likely to be an evil demon than the son of King Sām. Would you, pure and kind as you are, wish to take such a one for your husband or to pine away for love of him? Come, dearest of mistresses, there are handsome young princes enough in the world whose parentage is in no doubt.'

But Rudāba was affronted that, even from goodwill to her, they should speak slightingly of Zāl, and she said sharply in reply, 'You talk nonsense. With what other husband in the world could I be satisfied, once I had loved Zāl? If I have set my heart on the brightest and most beautiful of all the most distant stars, shall I be content with the pale, waning moon? I am not asking for the Caesar, the lord of the Lands of the West, nor for the Emperor of Turān, nor yet for Great King Minucher as my husband; but only for the son of Sām, who is a king no greater and no more powerful than my own father. As for the strange colour of his hair: what of it? People may call him an old man or a young boy, it makes no difference to my love for him.' And then, her proud words spoken, she began to weep.

When the five girls saw how deeply she loved, they forgot all prudence and sought only to help her to her desire. 'Tell no one else of this matter,' they warned her. And then they promised, 'Even if we have to learn spells from a sorcerer, and turn ourselves into swift gazelles, or birds that can fly through the air, we shall do so, if it is only by such means that we can win you Prince Zāl for a husband.'

Through her tears Rudāba smiled at them. 'Do this for me,' she said, 'and I shall be grateful to you—yes, and happy—for ever.'

The very next day Rudāba's five Turanian girls slipped unseen out of the palace and hurried down to the river. It was springtime and flowers—narcissus, lily, tulip, and jonquil—bloomed brightly and smelt sweetly along all the river's edge. When the girls came to a spot directly opposite Zāl's pavilion, they began to pick flowers, laughing and chattering together and calling to one another in voices loud and clear enough to reach across the water; and many a glance they cast towards the other bank.

Zāl, coming out of his pavilion, heard them and looked across the river. The happy laughter of the Turanian slaves brought sharply to his mind his own discontent, and his sorrow that he was never likely to meet with the fair princess for whom his heart longed. 'They are pretty girls, those who laugh and gather flowers yonder,' he said with a sigh. 'And Ormuzd has surely shown them grace, for they sound happy also. Who are they?'

Someone answered him, 'I understand, lord, that they are the favourite slaves of the Princess Rudāba, daughter of King Mehrāb.'

Zāl's melancholy vanished instantly. 'The favourite servants of Rudāba. Are they indeed?' he murmured to himself. Then he sent for his bow and quiver. He set an arrow to the bow and waited. Before long, disturbed by the girls, a wild duck rose up from the reeds on their side of the river and took wing. Quick as thought, Zāl loosed his arrow and the duck fell dead on the opposite bank, close by the girls. Calling to a tall, good-looking fellow from among those of his men who stood near by, Zāl ordered him to cross the river and fetch the duck. At once the man rowed over; and the girls, far from retiring modestly with downcast eyes until he had taken the duck and gone, crowded around the dead bird, praising aloud the skill of the marksman who had brought it down. When the man approached, one of them smiled at him and said, 'Tell us, stranger, who is that handsome young man who shot at the duck? He shoots straight and fast and seems, from his looks and bearing, to be a fine lord.'

'Fine lord he certainly is,' replied the man. 'He is my master Zāl, son of Sām, king of Zābulestān. And, as you say, handsome he is indeed. And truly, I would say that for beauty of face and form, there is none in all the world, man or woman, to equal him.'

The five girls exclaimed at this with mock indignation, and the one who had spoken before laughed and said, 'That cannot be, stranger, for in the palace of King Mehrāb lives one more beautiful by far than any other, his daughter and our mistress, the Princess Rudāba.'

The man shook his head. 'Nay, whoever she may be, she could not be more beautiful than Prince Zāl.'

'Were they to meet and stand beside each other, your master and our mistress,' said the girl, 'then we could see which of us was the liar, you or I.'

Another of the girls said with a sigh, 'What a marriage it would be, between the two fairest lovers in all the world. By my word, if your boasting has any truth in it, your Prince Zāl must be the only man living who would be a worthy husband for our princess.'

'I will tell him that,' laughed the man. He picked up the duck and rowed back across the river; and with many satisfied smiles and many glances of triumph, each to the other, the girls busied themselves with more flower-gathering, and waited hopefully.

When Zāl was told of what the slave-girls had said, he was delighted that things had gone even better than he had dared to hope. He sent at once for the treasure chests he carried with him on his journeying and, opening them, quickly chose out jewels and gold—bracelets of turquoise and cornelian, crystal ear-rings, necklaces with pendants of lapis lazuli and iridescent shell—rich gifts for the princess of Kābulestān. These gems he dispatched across the river to the Turanian girls, bidding them carry to their mistress his gifts and his respectful greetings.

Carefully concealing Zāl's gifts among the flowers they had picked, each with two great armfuls of spring blossoms, the girls ran back to the palace. At the door of Rudāba's apartments the porter grumbled at them. 'Shameless hussies, slyly running off down to the river when there are strangers encamped on the other side.

Picking flowers indeed! It is more likely by far that you went to make eyes over the water at the prince of Zābulestān's men.'

'Do not be cross with us, old one,' coaxed the girls, 'for it is spring, the time for youth and happiness.'

Rudāba took Zāl's gifts and listened to every word that the girls had to tell her of him, all five of them talking at once and all loud in his praise. Rudāba laughed. 'So you have changed your tune now that you have seen him. What of the white-haired old man, fallen from a bird's nest, against whom you warned me so earnestly?' Happily she smiled at them all. 'Dear, good friends, you have my thanks for what you have done for me today, and you will be well rewarded. But first, let two of you go again to the river and contrive to send a message to the prince for me. Tell him that I have received his gifts and would now see him, face to face, that I may thank him for them. Off with you, as fast as you may, and let the other three of you help me to prepare to greet him.'

And so, while two of the girls carried their mistress's message to Zāl, bidding him come to Rudāba secretly, after dark, the others made ready their mistress's apartments, decking them with costly hangings and strewing everywhere the flowers they had gathered that morning.

Zāl waited impatiently, and as soon as it was dusk, he crossed the river attended by only a few well-trusted followers, and made his way as the girls had directed him, to that tower where Rudāba's apartments were.

Rudāba, with her Turanian girls, had gone up to the flat roof of the palace to watch for him, and as soon as the girls espied the little group of men coming cautiously towards the tower in the dusk, they told their mistress. Excitedly Rudāba went to the parapet and called down softly, 'Welcome, honoured son of Sām.' Now that it had come almost to the moment of their meeting, she was suddenly shy, and appalled by her own boldness.

Zāl called up to her, 'Princess fairer than the moon, I, who through many heavy days, have waited and prayed for this moment, greet you.'

'You have come on foot from the river, noble prince. You will be weary and in need of refreshment and rest. Come up to me. See, here is a ladder for you to climb.' And she let fall her plait of dark hair, so that it tumbled down over the side of the tower like a rope.

But Zāl only raised the ends of the long tresses to his lips and kissed them gently. 'No,' he said, 'that would be too frail a ladder, and one of which I am unworthy.' He took from an attendant a rope and cast its end upwards. The princess caught it and made it fast to the stonework of the tower, and Zāl climbed up to her. She took him by the hand and led him down into her apartments, and there by lamplight they saw each other at last, and both knew that they had not been mistaken in supposing themselves in love. They embraced in great joy and swore to be true for ever.

When Mehrāb learnt of his daughter's love for Zāl, he was well pleased, and he received Zāl willingly as Rudāba's husband. But Zāl knew that his marriage with the daughter of a king whose good faith could not be trusted, and who was of the line of Zohāk the monster, would be received with anger by his father; and would, moreover, be unwelcome to the Great King Minucher. So he and Rudāba were married secretly, and only Mehrāb and a few of his more favoured courtiers and servants knew of it.

7: The Birth and Boyhood of Rustem

ZĀL and Rudāba had great joy of each other's love; but, though she was happy and content enough with matters as they were, Zāl regretted that his marriage had to be kept secret, and that he had to divide his days between his duties in his own land of Zābulestān and his lovely wife in Kābul. He longed to see Rudāba at his side each day, and he would have liked to tell all the world that the beautiful daughter of Mehrāb was his wife. His regret was increased a hundred-fold when he and Rudāba knew that a child was to be born to them, and he might not share the good tidings with even his father, Sām.

But these small trials were as nothing when weighed against the anxiety and grief that came to him when, one day around the time that their child was to be born, word was brought to him in Zābul that Rudāba was gravely ill. He left Sām's palace at once, almost forgetting, in his apprehension, all need for secrecy and caution, and rode like one crazed for the city of Kābul. He found Rudāba in a high fever, with all the physicians in Kābulestān—sent for in haste by King Mehrāb—gathered about her couch, shaking their heads and whispering together ineffectually, as, one after the other, each failed to find a cure for her sickness. Mehrāb himself was bowed down by grief and could only weep and wring his hands. In vain Zāl pleaded with the physicians, in vain he threatened them; one and all they declared themselves powerless to save his wife. In anguish, Zāl sat at Rudāba's bedside, her burning hand in his, and watched her dying. 'Was it only to suffer thus,' he wondered, 'that I left the Simurgh's nest and came to live as a man?' Then in an instant he had remembered the Simurgh's parting promise and the feather which she had given him and which he always carried with him, safely within an amulet.

He unloosed Rudāba's hand and stood up, suddenly hopeful. To Mehrāb, who still wept close by, he showed the feather, and Mehrāb, too, became less despairing. They sent for a brazier and Zāl dropped the feather on to the glowing charcoal. It curled up and vanished, quite burnt away. For a long, heart-tearing moment there was no sign, then suddenly everything in Rudāba's chamber was dim and indistinct as though under a dark cloud—and then the Simurgh folded her black wings and daylight returned. 'What ails you, my nurseling?' she asked.

'My Rudāba, my dearest wife, is dying.'

'Have no fear, for she will not die. It is destined that you and she together will, with happiness, watch your son grow up. In all the world there will be none like him. Lion-limbed in strength and lion-hearted in courage, his fame will stretch far and all men will respect his name.'

Then the Simurgh told them how to brew a soothing draught for Rudāba, so that her fever was eased, and she fell into a deep and gentle sleep. Under the Simurgh's direction, the physicians—who alone had been able to do nothing for her—tended her; and when she awoke, with all signs of sickness past, it was to hear the cries of her son, who already, at his birth, seemed bigger and stronger than any other new-born child had ever been. With joy Zāl and Rudāba saw his vigorous movements and heard his noisy demands for milk; and it seemed to them that such a fine, strong boy would indeed grow up to be everything that the Simurgh had foretold. With all their hearts they thanked her; and before she spread her wings and vanished from their sight, she plucked another feather and gave it to Zāl. 'When you again have need of me,' she said, 'I shall come to you.'

Zāl named his son Rustem and the child grew fast, first to a strong and sturdy boy and then to a tall, broad-shouldered youth who knew no fear of anything, neither man nor beast, neither good spirit nor evil demon. Zāl was so proud of his son that he soon no longer sought to keep secret from his father and all others the truth about his marriage to Rudāba and the birth of the boy. And on seeing how fine a grandson he had, Sām, so far from being displeased, gave to Rustem his own huge battle-mace, so heavy that no man but Sām himself could wield it, declaring himself certain that it would not be long before the boy could lift it unaided.

So fast did Rustem grow, and so tall and strong was he for his years, that all men far and near—whether they had set eyes on him or not—soon spoke of Zāl's son, and many were the fanciful tales that were told of Rustem, both then and ever after: how on the day he was weaned he ate bread and meat enough to satisfy five grown men; that he became taller than eight tall men, each standing on the shoulders of another; how at no more than the sound of his voice, leopards died of fear; that his strength was the strength not of a man, but of an elephant; how with just one finger he could cast a stone two leagues or more; and how, if he but stamped upon hard rock, his foot sank into it as though it were precarious sand.

These tales and many others were soon on all men's lips. Yet even if these many tales were wider than the truth, Rustem was indeed strong, and he was soon able to wield his grandfather's mace with as good effect as Sām himself, as he proved in his earliest adventure.

One night, not long after Sām had handed over to Zāl the kingship of Zābulestān, Rustem was awoken by the noise of some great excitement in the palace. Boyishly eager to know what was afoot, he jumped up and ran from his apartments to find out for himself. He discovered a great uproar, with guards and servants hurrying everywhere. It seemed that the king's white elephant had run mad and broken his chain. 'He has trampled several men to death already,' Rustem was told. 'And now no one dare approach him. We must rouse the king and tell him of it.'

'No!' exclaimed Rustem impetuously. 'There is no need to awaken my father. I will deal with the matter myself. You may tell him of it in the morning.' He ran back to his apartments for Sām's battle-mace and then hurried towards the stables where the royal elephants were housed. From over the stable walls he could hear the frantic trumpeting of the crazed beast and the terrified screaming of the other elephants, the splintering of wood and the falling of bricks, as the white elephant wrecked the stable buildings. It was plain that it would not be long before the huge creature broke down the gate of the stables to rage about the palace, destroying everything and everybody in its path.

The one trembling guard who still stood at his post before the gate refused to let Rustem through. 'No man could face that elephant and live, young master. If you enter the stables you will be killed, as surely as I live. And how should I dare to face the king and tell him that I allowed you to go to your death?' And the man set himself firmly in Rustem's way.

But Rustem paid the guard no heed. With one blow of his fist the boy sent him sprawling senseless to the ground. Then, breaking open the barred and bolted gate with Sām's mace, he ran through. In the stable courtyard there was destruction everywhere: fallen masonry, broken timbers, several elephants dead and the others cowering in terror, and the trampled bodies of the elephant-keepers; and in the midst of it all the enormous white elephant towering like a hill above the havoc it had caused.

When it saw Rustem it trumpeted furiously and charged at him, an immense, rocking mass. Rustem, without hesitation, roaring out

his defiance at the top of his young, shrill voice, ran straight at the elephant, raising the mace as he went and swinging it above his head. They came together, boy and elephant, with a crash that shook the palace like an earthquake; and as the mace smashed the elephant's skull, the great beast fell dead.

To the bunch of agitated and fearful guards and servants which had followed him, fearing for his safety, Rustem only smiled cheerfully, well pleased with himself, and said, 'I told you that there was no need to awaken the king, and that I could settle the matter for you.' While they stared unbelievingly from their young master to the dead elephant, Rustem shouldered his mace and returned to his apartments to finish his disturbed night's sleep.

8: How Rustem Found Raksh

THE rivalry and enmity between the Persian empire and its subject kingdoms on one hand, and, on the other, the empire of Turān and those lands allied to it, which had begun during the reigns of Iraj and his envious brother Tur, continued down the generations. And although the two countries were not always at open war, it was but rarely that they could be said to be at peace. The Caesars, the rulers of the Lands of the West, the one-time empire of Salm, also had no love for the Great Kings of Persia; but the Lands of the West lay farther off, and so were less of a threat than Turān.

During the reign of Minucher, Turān had little chance of succeeding in battle. Against an empire ruled by one so skilled in the stratagems of war as was Minucher, and protected by a well-drilled army led by that same fine warrior, Turān had only brief victories and few; but after the death of Minucher the rulers of Turān felt stronger and their hopes of victory over Persia rose higher. The Emperor Pesheng, who ruled in Turān at the time of Minucher's death, began a long and sometimes successful campaign against Persia, giving charge of the Turanian army to his son, Afrāsib, a brave and daring leader, who sorely harried the Persians.

Not many years after Rustem had slain Zāl's white elephant, he went to his father, though still little more than a boy, and asked leave to lead an army of the men of Zābulestān against Afrāsib. But Zāl, though he had no doubts of Rustem's courage, was less confident of his battle-skill, and he replied, 'My son, as you have reminded me, it was you, alone and unaided, who slew the white elephant. Yet one beast, however large and however dangerous, is a very different matter from the Turanian army led by men so practised in battle as Afrāsib and his generals. I do not think you old enough, nor have you had the experience needed, for me to allow you to risk your life—and the lives of the men of Zābulestān. For a good leader reckons victory not only by the number of dead enemies, but by the number of his own dead, also. I would have you wait a year or two, until you are older and know more of battle-craft. Now is that time in your life for feasting and entertainment, for music and poetry and song; for you to disport yourself and drink deep and, if you will, fall in love. The labours of battle and the duties of leadership will come to you quite soon enough. And when they do come,

I have no doubt that you will prove yourself a most mighty warrior, and one whose fame will stretch far and wide. But those things are for tomorrow, my son. Today, be young at heart and enjoy life to the full without cares.'

'My father,' said Rustem, 'these broad shoulders of mine grew to bear the weight of armour, not to be decked with silk and jewels. These big hands were formed to carry a sword and a battle-mace, not a wine cup or a harp. And truly, I have little love for music or poetry. The music my ears long for is the neighing of war-horses; and the songs to please me best are the battle-cries of brave men who follow where I lead them.'

He pleaded so earnestly that at last Zāl yielded and gave leave for Rustem to go to war. Rustem was overjoyed and began to make ready at once. 'I have a sword second to none, and a fine bow, and I have the battle-mace of my grandfather Sām,' he said, his eyes bright with his eagerness. 'Now all I need is a horse to carry me into battle. My war-horse must be strong enough to bear me fully armed for hour after hour—indeed, for day after day—and it must be fearless and high-mettled and swift besides. Yet strength and courage and spirit and speed are not enough. Rustem's war-horse must have quick understanding also, and patience and calmness when they are needed.'

Neither in his own nor in his father's stables was there a horse with all these qualities, so Rustem sent to the horse-dealers of Zābulestān, bidding them bring him the finest horses from their droves. But the horses which they brought to the palace, though proud-stepping and swift enough, were showy beasts picked out for their looks as being worthy to carry a prince, as much as for the other qualities which Rustem required of a mount. After several days of disappointment, Rustem thought, 'This is no way for me to choose my horse, to have it chosen for me by other men. I must see for myself every horse, and not only those which their drovers think that I should see.'

So Rustem went about Zābulestān with only a few attendants, and not giving it out that he was the prince; and everywhere there was a herd of horses, he had them driven past him—every horse in every herd—and whenever he saw a likely mount he called out to the drovers and they caught it and brought it to him, applauding his choice and ready with their praises of the beast, bidding him observe its fine head or its strong withers, or its sturdy quarters. But Rustem paid no heed to their words. He only pressed with his hand upon the back of each horse that was brought to him, and the back of each one of them was bent beneath his hand until its belly touched the ground; and Rustem had to shake his head and say, 'Take it away. If it cannot support the weight of only one of my hands, how could it carry me? Take it away, it is not for me.'

In this manner Rustem saw every horse in Zābulestān and found none to his liking. He travelled then—still as though he were a young man of substance but of no great rank—into Kābulestān, to the horse-dealers of that country. And there, in his mother's land, he at last found what he sought.

In a certain herd of horses, as they were driven past him one by one, there was a bay mare which stood higher than the others by several hands. Strong-limbed and swift, with sharp-pricked ears, she was a powerful and noble beast. Beside her ran her foal, a colt of two years, as tall and powerful as his dam, and of a light, bright, golden colour, dappled with red. The sharp eyes in the fine head he held so high were black and fierce, his mane was a ripple of flame and his tail curved proudly. The moment that he caught sight of him, Rustem pointed to this colt. 'There is my horse!' he exclaimed excitedly. 'Bring him to me.'

But the chief drover, standing beside him, shook his head. 'No, sir, choose any horse but that one. That is Raksh and he belongs to another. Do not, I beg of you, seek to take another man's horse.'

'There is no brand-mark on him,' objected Rustem. 'Why should that be so, if he already belongs to another? And to whom does he belong, this Raksh? I want him for myself.'

'Let him be, sir,' pleaded the drover. 'He is named Raksh, but we drovers like to call him Rustem's Raksh, for so fiery and strong and noble a mount deserves to carry a man no less in stature than a giant, as Prince Rustem of Zābulestān is said to be. Forgive me, sir, but though you are as tall and fine and broad a man as any I have ever seen—or am ever like to see, unless Prince Rustem comes this way: and why should he?—you are no giant. Besides, other men than you, sir, have had a fancy to own this horse. But when they would have mounted him, he has flung them to the ground disdainfully. And his dam, also, has resisted and fought like a very lioness in defence of her foal. Between them, sir, they have worsted every would-be master.'

Rustem gave a huge, delighted laugh. 'If you will not bring him to me, then I must catch him for myself.' He snatched from the drover the noosed rope which the man held and, swinging it about

his head, he flung it with true aim about the neck of the colt and pulled it taut. Instantly, while her colt stood firm as a rock, the mare gave a wild whinny. Then, with ears laid flat and hooves flashing, she charged at Rustem in such a manner that any man could have been forgiven for loosing the rope which held the foal, and running off as fast as his legs could carry him. Indeed, the chief drover and those of his men who stood near by, fled to a safe distance and looked on from there. But Rustem stood his ground, holding fast and firmly to the rope; and as the mare came upon him, he gave a great shout of defiance, like the roar of a lion. The mare stopped dead, falling back upon her haunches as though suddenly reined in by the hand of an unseen rider; then she slowly backed away, prudently retreating, yet still eyeing Rustem threateningly.

Rustem pulled on the rope and drew the colt inch by inch towards him; though the colt came none too willingly, his ears laid back and with his black eyes flashing. When the beast was near enough, Rustem laid his hand upon his back and pressed downwards with all his might. The strong spine did not yield by a hair's breadth. With one leap Rustem sprang upon the colt's back, and it was as though the beast felt his great weight as no more than the weight of a fly. Yet he made no attempt to throw Rustem, but grew of a sudden calm and docile, for all the world as though Rustem's Raksh had recognized Rustem, now that he was come at last.

Rustem called the chief drover back to him. 'Do not look so puzzled, my friend. I am Rustem himself and I have come to claim my Raksh. Well have you kept him for me and cared for him until this day, and I thank you for it with all my heart. Now tell me his price, for I am eager to call him mine in truth.'

With tears of joy the drover answered, 'To you, Prince Rustem, he has no price. He is yours, as he has been since the day he was foaled. Yet if you would pay for him, let his price be the freeing of Persia from the hosts of Turān. Take him, lord prince, and may he carry you to victory against our enemies.'

So Raksh was saddled and bridled and joyfully Rustem rode home to the city of Zābul; and on that day began a friendship between man and horse which ended only on the day they died.

9: Rustem's Journey to Māzendarān

HAVING won his father's permission, and having found the warhorse he had set his heart upon, Rustem, on Raksh, rode off to join the imperial army. He was welcomed by the Great King, and went out to battle at once, too keen for fighting to delay a day longer than he needed. The eager youth soon proved himself the equal of every older and well-tried warrior; and his comrades on the battlefield soon accepted him as the best among them. Few though his years were, they gave him ungrudging respect and admiration, and all felt a true affection for the young warrior whose huge stature and bulk should have made him clumsy and awkward—but did not—and whose greatest joy seemed to be in the din and press of battle.

The campaign against the Turanian invaders lasted long. It dragged its unhappy, bloody way into first months, then years; and neither side gained any decisive victory. Yet, once Rustem had joined the forces of Persia, the Great King's successes soon begun to outnumber those of his enemies. In the field of battle, wherever Rustem fought, there the Persians were certain to be gaining ground.

Rustem was a fearless fighter, never caring against how skilled an antagonist he fought, or against how many at one time; and very swiftly word of the young Persian champion had spread to the Turanian ranks. Before long his fame was as great among the enemy as it was among his own comrades, and even the bravest Turanian warrior felt his heart shiver in his breast at the name of Rustem, son of Zāl. His proud and independent spirit, his occasional quick outbursts of rage when roused, and his good-natured generosity—as well as the multitude of tales that were told of his strength and skill—became as familiar to the Turanians as they were among his fellow-countrymen; and that to men who had not even glimpsed him on the battlefield. Those few Turanian warriors who had met and fought with him, and yet lived to remember it, remembered it with dread, and prayed that they might not meet with him again. On the Persian side, when men were hard pressed or in peril, they would say, 'Send for Rustem, and all will be well,' such was the reliance they placed on him.

The years passed and Rustem grew to manhood. Persian victories became more frequent, and the Turanians retreated back beyond the River Oxus. The big campaign was over, though there were still skirmishes and raids here and there along the borderlands; and no one, on either side, expected or believed in any lasting peace between the two great empires. But many warriors, both Persian and Turanian, were free to return home; and subject-kings led their own small armies back to their own lands and took up again the task of ruling their own people. There were once more courtiers and lords and generals at the Great King's court; and champions who, like Rustem, fretted if they were too long away from battle, travelled in search of adventure—and sometimes found it.

One of Rustem's most dangerous adventures happened at this time: his journey to Māzendarān and his combat with the White Demon. This is how it came about.

The wide empire of the Persians was then ruled by Kāvus, who had but lately succeeded to the throne and tiara of the Great King, and King of Kings. As monarchs are judged, he was no wicked ruler; but, stubborn and self-admiring, he was a man lacking in that wisdom which should be a king's, and one who too often acted with stupidity.

On the borders of the empire, encircled and protected by seven mountains, there lay the kingdom of Māzendarān. Little was known of this land, and that little was not good. It was said to be a country where only demons dwelt and the power of Ahrimān was strong. This was, indeed, not far from the truth, for the king of Māzendarān was a sorcerer, who lived under the protection of the White Demon of the Seven Mountains, an evil creature much beloved of Ahrimān.

One day a travelling musician came to the Persian capital and presented himself at the palace of the Great King. Kāvus made him welcome, and bade him play and sing for the pleasure of the court. Now, this musician was in reality a demon in man's shape, sent by his master the White Demon, at the command of Ahrimān, who wished thereby to destroy the Great King, together with his army, by tempting him into Māzendarān. Plucking delicately at the strings of his arched-harp, in a sweet, melodious voice, the demon sang of the beauties and delights of the city of Māzendarān: the joyful folk who lived there, the lovely women, the fine buildings, and the heaps of treasure, piled high, which lay in the streets of Māzendarān for the taking.

Kāvus listened, spellbound, to the song; and when the singing was done, he exclaimed, 'I must see so fair a place with my own eyes.' His counsellors cried out against such folly, reminding him of other, darker things which were told of Māzendarān. But Kāvus, with a gesture, swept aside their warnings, saying, 'The monarch of so rich a city should be my subject and pay tribute. Consider the many coffers which the tribute-money from Māzendarān would fill. I shall lead an army against Māzendarān, and it shall evermore be counted among the cities of my empire.' And in spite of the protests of his counsellors and generals, he ordered the imperial army to be made ready for the long march to Māzendarān.

Zāl, when he heard what was afoot, came hastily from Zābulestān, to join with the others in seeking to dissuade Kāvus from his purpose. But he, too, failed; and, shrugging his shoulders over the Great King's folly, he returned home. Even Rustem, in spite of his love of adventure, would have no part in so rash an undertaking. 'The Great King must be crazed or bewitched!' he said.

In due course Kāvus, with his army and his generals Gudarz and Tus, set out for Māzendarān. The way was long, for the city lay far off, but the going was easy and pleasant. The roads and the tracks were good, and the country through which they ran was fertile and well-watered, and the progress of the army went well, and, indeed, merrily; and by the time they reached the foot-hills of the Seven Mountains, beyond which lay their goal, even those who had advised against the campaign had forgotten their misgivings; while Kāvus himself was boastful, elated and full of confidence. The march had taken seven months; but they had lost neither man nor beast on the road, and all were in the best of spirits.

They halted at the mountains, and Kāvus sent Giv, the bold young son of Gudarz, ahead with a small group of men to spy out what lay before them. Giv returned with word of the city beyond the mountains. 'All is as the minstrel said,' he reported eagerly to Kāvus. 'The buildings are tall and magnificent, lovely women in fine robes walk in the streets, and all the folk wear jewels. It must indeed be the richest city in all the world.'

Kāvus gave the command, and the army set off over the mountain and down into the valley where the splendours and the beauties of Māzendarān lay spread out before them to dazzle their eyes and lend speed to their feet as they descended.

But as soon as word was brought to the sorcerer king of Māzendarān of the approach of the Great King and his army, he laughed, and sent for aid to his protector, the White Demon. From his cave in the mountains, the White Demon blew, and a terrible storm arose. Thunder, lightning, sleet and hail struck the invaders, who could

do nothing but cower beneath its blows, quite unable to protect themselves from this unexpected enemy. When the storm ceased, out of all the great army which had set out to conquer Māzendarān, only Kāvus, his generals and young Giv, and a few score warriors remained. Appalled and terrified, they looked about them at the devastation, the dead and dying men and beasts, the broken chariots and baggage wagons, and hid their eyes from it.

'If Māzendarān should attack us now,' said Kāvus, 'we are indeed lost. Oh, that Rustem were with us!' And he had wit enough to send a messenger back over the mountains to carry word to Zāl of their plight.

But worse was to come for the Persian survivors. The White Demon blew again and darkness fell upon them—not the darkness of night, but the darkness of blindness—so that each man would have given all he possessed to be able, once again, to look even upon the dreadful sights which surrounded him.

The White Demon grinned in hideous joy. 'So they shall remain,' he said, 'until their eyes are bathed in the blood of my heart and my liver. And when will that be? Why, never!' And he and the sorcerer king laughed long together. But Kāvus and the others could only grope their way about the valley, grubbing up herbs and roots to eat, caught in the prison of blindness and fenced in by the mountain slopes.

It was almost a year after Kāvus had set out, eager for conquest and spoils, that his weary messenger reached the city of Zābul with his cry for help. Rustem did not hesitate. He ordered Raksh to be saddled and he made ready at once to set off. But as he was putting on his bronze-plated helmet with its fine silver decoration and his mailed jacket, he said doubtfully to Zāl, 'If it took the Great King half a year to reach Māzendarān, even though Raksh gallop like the wind, I cannot make the journey in less than a third of that time, and I fear I may well come to Māzendarān too late.'

After a moment's hesitation, Zāl said unwillingly, 'There are two roads to Māzendarān. One is long and easy, and that way the army went. The other is short and would take a man on a fast horse no more than fourteen days. Yet it is beset with perils for every step of the way.'

'Who cares for perils, when speed is required?' said Rustem, flinging about him his favourite cloak, made from the skin of a huge leopard. 'Tell me where this road runs, my father, and I will take it.'

Rudāba began to weep. 'I shall never see you again, my son.'

Rustem put his arms about her. 'Dry your tears, dearest of mothers. The shorter the path to Māzendarān, the sooner you will welcome me home. Have no doubt of it.'

Raksh was brought, ready saddled and bridled. His saddle-cloth was of leopard-skin, and his harness was decorated with silver and bronze. Rustem hung his bow and quiver and a coiled length of strong rope from the saddlebow, and listened while Zāl told him in which direction he must ride, to find himself on the shorter road to Māzendarān. His huge iron sword in his grasp, and Sām's heavy battle-mace to hand, Rustem took leave of Zāl and Rudāba, leapt on to the back of the impatient Raksh, and was away, with a wave of his hand and a cheerful word flung over his shoulder to his anxious parents. 'Come now, make haste, my Raksh,' he said then. 'We have no time to lose.'

For two days and the night which lay between them, Rustem rode on, along the way to which Zāl had directed him; and at sunset on the second day he paused to rest near a water-hole in the midst of an open plain. From among a herd of wild asses which grazed there, he shot one and built a fire to cook it by. After he had eaten, he lay down to sleep in the shelter of a reed-bed; and Raksh lay down near by.

Now, it happened that Rustem had chosen to rest in the very spot where a lion had its lair; and before he had been long asleep, the lion returned from its hunting. Rustem still slept, but Raksh awoke instantly and was upon his feet, even as the lion gave its first angry growl at the intruders. As Raksh moved, the lion leapt upon him. Raksh flung the lion aside and, rearing up, struck at the beast with his forehooves. As the lion fell, Raksh bit at its back with his strong teeth, tearing at hide and mane. At the sound of their conflict, the furious neighing of Raksh and the roars of the lion, Rustem awoke in time to see Raksh trample the body of the dead lion into the ground.

'Raksh, good friend,' Rustem chided him, 'you should not have fought alone. It is only together that we have any hope of reaching Māzendarān, so you must take no risks. The next time danger threatens while I sleep, wake me, that we both may face it.'

In the morning they set off again, soon reaching the edge of a vast desert. Once more they travelled for two days and a night; yet after that time there still seemed no end to the desert which stretched all about them, no green or living thing in sight. Rustem had by this time dismounted and was leading the exhausted Raksh. The sand at his feet and the rocks over which he stumbled seemed to sway before him in the red light of the setting sun, which turned the whole world to a crimson sea. Yet it was not the desert which moved, but Rustem himself who swayed from side to side like a drunken man. Nostrils flaring and with drooping head, Raksh came heavily after him.

Rustem paused and closed his eyes to the sight of the wilderness. He leant his head against Raksh. 'This is the end of our journey, my Raksh.' He could only whisper the words through his parched and swollen lips. He slipped to his knees, his arms still about Raksh, believing that he would never rise again. A little later he opened his eyes, that he might die with a last defiant glance at the desert, the only enemy which had been able to overcome him, and he saw a plump sheep trot briskly by. At first he thought it a cruel trick played by the evening shadows as they lengthened swiftly from the rocks; but at a second glance, and a third, the sheep was still there, though fast trotting out of sight.

'Where there is a sheep so fat as that sheep is, there must be water close,' thought Rustem; and he rose and with renewed hope he struggled on as fast as he might, in the tracks of the sheep; and there, only a few hundred paces onward, amid sheltering rocks, lay a desert pool, fed by a stream, with the sheep at its edge, drinking.

As he and Raksh drank deeply, Rustem said, 'May you live long, O sheep, and never fall prey to leopard or lion, for you have saved our lives.'

By the time they had drunk their fill, darkness had fallen and Rustem and Raksh lay there beside the spring to sleep. 'Tonight, Raksh, rouse me should danger threaten. Do not face even a prowling jackal alone,' warned Rustem, as his eyes closed. But their night was peaceful and undisturbed.

For the fifth and sixth days Rustem travelled on, and in the evening of the sixth day he stopped to rest in a lonely, rocky place where he could see neither bird nor beast. But he found there a trickle of water coming from a rock, and a large cave to shelter him and Raksh. Rustem lay down, his eyes too weary to remain open another minute. To Raksh he said sleepily, 'Remember, wake me if even a jackal barks.'

Raksh lay down at the broad mouth of the cave and, like Rustem, was soon asleep. Yet he did not long remain undisturbed, for that cave was the den of a dragon, a magical beast which could vanish or appear at will. This dragon had been away from its den seeking prey, but now, its appetite satisfied, it returned to the cave to find Raksh asleep in its path. Furious, it scratched at the ground with one clawed foot and breathed upon Raksh. Raksh awoke instantly, to see an immense dragon glowing in the darkness beside him. Obedient to Rustem's command, Raksh did not attack the monster alone, but neighed shrilly and stamped to awaken Rustem. Rustem stirred, but instantly the dragon vanished, and when Rustem opened his eyes, it was to see only Raksh in the mouth of the cave, outlined against the night sky. He rose and looked around. 'I bade you rouse me for a prowling jackal, but I did not mean you to wake me to face the shadow of nothingness,' he grumbled sleepily. He lay down again, as did Raksh; and soon both were once more fast asleep.

The dragon re-appeared outside its cave, saw Raksh still there and roared angrily. Raksh awoke instantly and, as before, roused Rustem. But again the dragon vanished before Rustem set eyes on it. Sword in hand he peered around him into the darkness outside the cave, and saw nothing. 'What ails you, Raksh? Can you not let me rest?' Annoyed, he lay down and slept again.

A third time the dragon appeared; a third time Raksh awoke; and a third time he roused Rustem. But again the dragon had vanished. Rustem's temper flared up, and he shouted at Raksh, 'If you wake me once again tonight, it will be the worse for you. You have my word on that.'

A fourth time the dragon came; and this time Raksh hesitated, unable both to obey Rustem's order and to heed his threat, and he backed silently into the cave towards the spot where Rustem lay. This was the dragon's undoing, for the great monster followed Raksh into its den, confidently believing itself to have only one enemy to face.

Raksh stood over Rustem, still hesitating, and the dragon came nearer, its burning eyes lighting up the darkness of the cave. Raksh hesitated no longer. He gave a loud, threatening neigh and stamped upon the floor of the cave around Rustem's head, shaking the rocky walls. This time Rustem awoke to see the dragon. He snatched up his sword, and he and Raksh fell upon the monster at once, Raksh pounding with his hooves and biting, and Rustem with many swift strokes of his heavy sword.

The dragon, too enraged at being thus set upon in its own den, did not choose to vanish, but cried out, 'What puny, crawling things are you who dare to stand and face me? For centuries I have dwelt here undisturbed by any living creature. Why, the high-flying eagles do not presume to pass above this place, and even the very stars do not look down on it. Short lives will your impudence have brought you.' Roaring horribly, it attacked; but, hemmed in by the walls of the cave, it was no match for the two of them; and though their combat was terrible and death drew very close to them, Rustem and Raksh were the victors in the end. They had survived the third peril of their journey.

Again for two days and the night that parted them, Rustem and Raksh travelled on; and at evening on their eighth day of travelling, in the midst of a drear and arid wasteland, they came upon a group of green and leafy trees beside a pool of clear water. In the shade of the trees was a fair cloth spread upon the ground, and upon the cloth, bread and meat and fruits of every kind, with a jar of wine and a cup. Beside this feast lay soft cushions, and beside the cushions, a lute.

'This is undoubtedly some enchantment,' said Rustem. 'But I am not one to forgo a feast, enchanted though it be.' He dismounted and he and Raksh drank from the spring; then, while Raksh gratefully cropped the green plants which grew by the water, Rustem made a good meal off the fine fare provided—but with a wary glance about him all the time, lest he might be eating and drinking and taking his ease in a trap laid for his catching. But he was undisturbed, and everything was still and quiet.

All the good food gone, Rustem refilled the cup and took up the lute. 'As all know, I am but a sorry musician,' he said with a chuckle. 'Yet, since there is no one here to pass judgement on my playing, I shall cheer the desert with a song.' And he strummed on the lute-strings and sang a merry song of his own composing, just as the words came into his mind. As he was finishing his song, he was suddenly aware that he had another companion besides Raksh. On the cushions by him sat a fair young woman, slender and richly clad, who smiled at him.

'Who are you, my pretty one? And is it your feast that I have eaten?' he asked; but she gave him no answer save her smile. Rustem poured the last of the wine and offered her the cup. 'The least I can do, if I have been your guest, is to share with you the little that remains. You must forgive my greed, for I was hungry. For your hospitality, may the divine lord, great Ormuzd, bless you and keep you, fair stranger.'

Immediately he pronounced the name of Ormuzd, the woman gave a shriek—for she was a witch—and took her own shape, that of a hideous, malevolent old hag. She opened her mouth to curse Rustem; but he was too quick for her, snatching up his sword as he jumped to his feet. She fled, screaming out her curses and her threats.

'Such vile beings are best destroyed,' said Rustem. From his saddle which lay close by, he took up the rope he had brought with him, uncoiled it, swung it above him and flung the noose over the witch's head and shoulders as she ran. He dragged her, still screaming her curses, towards him and with one stroke of his sword ended her evil life.

Rustem and Raksh rested that night beside the witch's enchanted spring beneath the trees, and they set off once more at dawn. Again for the space of two days and a night they galloped ceaselessly across dry and burning wastelands. Then, towards evening on the tenth day of their journey, they came in sight of fertile, cultivated land, around the walls of a village. Thankfully they left the desert behind them, and Rustem reined Raksh in to a walk while they both rejoiced at the sight of trees and growing crops. At a stream Rustem dismounted to drink, and Raksh began to browse upon the fresh green shoots in a field of barley.

A farmer, returning to the village after his day's toil in the fields, saw a huge yellow-gold horse trampling and cropping the young barley. Had he but paused to find the horse's rider and spoken to him with civility, there is no doubt that Rustem would have called Raksh from the field. But instead the farmer rushed upon Raksh, shouting furiously, and began to beat him with the hoe and spade he carried. Before even Raksh, surprised by this attack, could begin to defend himself, Rustem, hearing the farmer's shouts, looked up from washing himself in the stream to see a strange man striking Raksh about the head. With a lion-roar, Rustem ran at the man, seizing him by the ears and swinging him off the ground and shaking him with such force that the unfortunate farmer's ears were pulled off, and he ran screaming for help to the village.

The lord of the village was a young man named Aolād; and when the terrified farmer stammered out that there was a demon and his monster-steed destroying the crops and advancing on the village, Aolād called up his handful of armed followers and rode quickly out from the village. He saw Rustem and Raksh at once, and bravely riding alone towards Rustem, while his reluctant men hung back, he called out, 'I am Aolād, lord of this village. Who are you, who disturb our peace?'

'If you were to hear my name, little lordling Aolād, your blood would freeze in terror,' Rustem called in reply. Jumping upon Raksh's back and flourishing his sword, he rode at Aolād. One and all, Aolād's followers fled; but the young man stood his ground for a few, fearful moments. Yet even he, as Rustem and Raksh bore down upon him, dared face certain death no longer. He turned his horse's head and made for the safety of the village walls. Rustem uncoiled his noosed rope and flung it about him, pinning his arms to his sides and unhorsing him.

Standing over Aolād, Rustem demanded, 'Do you know the fastest roads to Māzendarān and to the lair of the White Demon?'

Aolād nodded. 'I do indeed, and would willingly take neither.'

'If you would have me spare your life, young man, give me your promise to guide me to Māzendarān and the White Demon.'

'To Māzendarān I will guide you, but not to the White Demon. You cannot know what you ask of me. Only a madman would seek out the White Demon. His body is like a mountain, and it is said that those mountains among which he dwells are as little hills to him and they tremble at his feet.'

Rustem raised his sword. 'To Māzendarān and to the White Demon, or that is your last breath which you now take.'

'I have no choice,' said Aolād. 'It will be death for me, either way. To Māzendarān and the White Demon it shall be, and may Ormuzd protect us.'

Rustem sheathed his sword. 'Guide me faithfully, and I will make you king of Māzendarān. By all accounts, it is a city well worth ruling.'

'You are indeed a madman,' said Aolād. 'And I am no better, that I do not choose a quick and easy death at your hands this very minute.'

Rustem tied Aolād to a tree and slept undisturbed by the trembling villagers; and at dawn they set off, Aolād riding ahead, still bound by Rustem's rope, with Rustem holding to its end; since Rustem was taking no chances of his attempting to escape. After two days' journeying in this manner, they were at the foot of the Seven Mountains; and another two days passed before they were riding down into the valley where the blinded Persian survivors were prisoned. Fourteen days to the very hour of his starting out, Rustem was being embraced, with tears of joy and relief, by Kāvus and the others.

The next day, with many misgivings, Aolād led Rustem up the secret mountain path on the farther side of the valley, to the home of the White Demon, a huge cave, its entrance guarded by scores of lesser demons, all busy tending fires, preparing food, sharpening swords, and polishing weapons and armour. Even Rustem felt a little doubtful of his chances of winning past this horde of hideous creatures of Ahrimān to reach the cave and the White Demon himself. But Aolād said, 'At midday they will lie down to rest and sleep. It is ever their custom. Then, and then only, can you risk an attack upon the cave.'

Rustem looked up at the sun. 'There is yet an hour or two before midday. Until then, it shall be my turn to rest.' And he calmly lay down and went peacefully to sleep—yet not before he had tied Aolād firmly to a rock. 'Having come with me so far, it would be a pity that you should lose your promised kingdom, now the end is in sight,' he had said with a laugh, as he tightened the knots.

At midday, as Aolād had told him, the demons settled down to rest and soon were sleeping, all save the guards who stood just within the mouth of the cave, guarding their master's rest. With glances of disgust, Rustem picked his way carefully among the sprawled and snoring demons and reached the entrance to the cave before the guards espied him. At the very moment that they saw him, he rushed upon them, striking to either side of him with his sword and cutting down a demon at each stroke. In no time at all he was in the chamber of the White Demon himself, while behind him lay all the demon guards, each one of them dead or dying.

The cave was dark and stinking, but as soon as Rustem's eyes grew used to the darkness and he could see about him, he made out the huge shape of the White Demon lying in a corner from which earth-trembling snores were coming. Rustem, thinking it shameful to slay even a vile demon while he slept, roared out a challenge which echoed through the cave. The White Demon awoke and rose, and with a roar far surpassing Rustem's, came at him. The first stroke of Rustem's sword cut off one of the White Demon's hands. The second cut off one of his feet. But by then the White Demon was upon Rustem, still as powerful as fifty strong men, even lacking a foot and a hand. He grasped Rustem and crushed him against his huge body until Rustem thought that all his bones were surely broken. Yet he struggled and twisted in the darkness, his sword fallen to the ground, and only his hands and arms to fight with at such close quarters, and his feet slipping in the blood which poured from the White Demon's severed limbs. At last, just when it seemed to Rustem that he could resist not a moment longer, the White Demon began to weaken. With renewed hope and strength, Rustem raised him up above his head to the very roof of the cave and dashed him to the ground, where he lay still.

Weary but triumphant, Rustem dragged the body of the White Demon to the mouth of the cave. All the lesser demons, who had been wakened from their sleep by the sounds of combat, cried out in terror at the sight of their dead master, and turning, fled far away, never again to be seen in the Seven Mountains.

With his sword, Rustem hacked open the huge and hideous body and cut out the heart and liver. When the task was done, he was standing in an ever-spreading lake of demon-blood. With disgust he took up the heart and liver and went back to Aolād and Raksh and Aolād's terrified horse. 'It is over,' he said. 'Praise and thanks be to Ormuzd.' He untied Aolād and together they returned to where Kāvus and the other Persians waited. Into the eyes of each blinded man Rustem poured two drops of blood from the heart and the liver of the White Demon, and instantly his sight was restored.

With Kāvus and Rustem riding at their head, the few—but elated and triumphant—Persian warriors rode into Māzendarān and found that the sorcerer king had fled with his warriors. Kāvus feasted his victory for seven days; then he sent a messenger to where the sorcerer king lay hidden in the foot-hills, proclaiming him a subject-ruler and demanding annual tribute from Māzendarān. This the king refused. He led his men back and endeavoured to retake his city. In the battle that followed, Rustem did great deeds, worthy of a hundred men—which was as well, since the Persians were greatly outnumbered—and at last came face to face with the sorcerer king himself. At Rustem's attack the king changed himself into a huge rock against which Rustem's sword struck harmlessly. Furious, Rustem flung down his sword, lifted the rock high above his head and shouted, 'Take human shape, O evil one, or I shall dash you to little chips of stone!'

The sorcerer king became a thick, dark cloud inside iron armour, and stood to face Rustem, who took up his sword again.

'In the name of Ormuzd, Rustem,' cried Kāvus, 'kill him, if you can!'

Rustem raised his sword and, with one blow, sliced armour and cloud in two. And so ended the sorcerer king of Māzendarān.

Kāvus honoured the promise of Rustem, and gave Māzendarān to Aolād, who ruled long and well as a subject-king of the great empire of Persia.

10: Rustem and Tahmina

ONE day at a time when the warfare between Persia and Turān had slackened for a season and Rustem was able to enjoy the pleasures of peace, he rode out on Raksh for a day's hunting. He took with him no attendants, for he wanted to be free for a while of both palace ceremonial and military formality; and he had with him no friend, since he had Raksh for company, and Rustem ever found in Raksh a companion as agreeable as any man—and better than most.

In his search for game worth hunting, quite knowingly he crossed the Persian borderland on to the plain of Turān, where that day there was game in plenty. He had soon brought down a plump antelope and, it being midday and the sun high in the sky, Rustem dismounted near a spring to eat and drink, and to rest himself and Raksh. He made a fire of brushwood and branches, then, pulling up a sapling by the roots, he spitted the antelope on it and set it to cook over the fire. When it was roasted, he ate every scrap of the meat with relish, even cracking open the bones to lick out the soft marrow. Then, leaving Raksh free to roam at will and graze where he would, Rustem lay down beneath a shady tree and soon was fast asleep.

Raksh was contentedly cropping the green leaves and sweet herbs at some distance from the place where Rustem lay, when a group of seven or eight Turanian horsemen came by. They were certain warriors in the service of the ruler of Samengān, a subject-king who paid tribute to Afrāsib, who had by then succeeded his father Pesheng as Emperor of Turān. As soon as these men caught sight of the huge horse with his strange, red-dappled, golden hide, they guessed him to be Raksh, the horse of Rustem, that feared and hated enemy of Turān; for the fame of Rustem's horse had spread almost as far as the fame of the Persian hero himself.

'What a prize Raksh would be for our king!' one of them exclaimed eagerly; and immediately they united in an attempt to catch him, flinging noosed ropes about his head and neck. Raksh, rearing high above his attackers and neighing in furious rage, killed three of the men before he was overcome. One man he kicked to death, another he trampled beneath his hooves, and he bit off the head of the third. Yet at last he was captured and bound. The men did not wait to see if Rustem were close by; with prudent speed they set off in triumph with their costly-won prize, eager to show Raksh to their king in the city of Samengān.

When Rustem awoke and called to Raksh and heard no instant whinny in reply, it seemed to him at once that all was not well with the horse. He followed the hoofprints of Raksh as he had wandered, grazing, from one patch of green herbage to another, until he reached a place where the shrubs and flowers and all growing things had been

trampled underfoot, while the very earth had been ground to dust, as though in a battle; and from that place the hoofprints of Raksh led away in the direction of the city of Samengān, with other tracks beside and over them. It was clear to Rustem what had happened while he slept, and he fell into a great rage, not only that he, the mightiest and most famed warrior in the world, had been robbed of his horse and left to trudge across the Turanian plain on foot, but because his beloved friend and loyal companion was lost. His temper worsening with each minute that passed, he strode off, following the tracks to the very gates of Samengān, where he shouted out to the guards that he was Rustem, son of Zāl, and demanded to see and speak with their king.

The guards escorted the furious Rustem to the palace, and there he stamped and shouted his way into the presence of the king, complaining that he had been robbed of Raksh, and declaring all the people of Samengān to be cowardly robbers who would steal from a sleeping man, and the warriors of Samengān to be no better than common horse-thieves, and loudly and imperiously demanding justice.

The king of Samengān, who knew well the benefit it would be to him to have the great Rustem as a friend rather than the enemy he was, greeted him with courtesy and smooth agreeableness, ignoring his anger and his rough manner. As though it were unknown to him, he deplored the loss of Raksh; and, though knowing full well where Raksh was at that very moment, promised to send out men to search everywhere in the city and all about the surrounding countryside for him, that he might restore Raksh to his most distinguished and welcome guest.

Rustem, who was unsure whether the king was lying or not, and appreciating the help he could undoubtedly offer in the search for Raksh—always supposing the king were not himself the thief—curbed his hot words a little and received the king's welcome and his promises with a certain amount of grace.

The king of Samengān ordered a banquet to be prepared immediately, with singers and musicians for the entertainment of his guest; and he himself waited upon Rustem, serving him with rich meats and choicest fruits and all manner of other delicacies, and pouring Rustem's wine with his own hands. When the time came for Rustem to retire to rest upon the soft bed that had been made ready for him, there was still no word of Raksh, though the king spoke assuredly and cheerfully of how his men would surely find the horse before the night was out, and of how he would have good tidings for his guest by dawn. He seemed so confident—as well he might have been, with Raksh all the time in his own stables—that Rustem had hope that he would indeed be as good as his word; and he lay down to rest and was soon fast asleep with as little fear for his safety as though he had been in his own palace, instead of several leagues into enemy territory.

At around midnight he awoke suddenly, with the good fighting man's instant return to full awareness, to find the room in which he lay softly lighted by a lamp held in the hands of a slave-girl, and to see, standing beside his couch, a lovely maiden in rich robes.

'Prince Rustem,' she said, 'I am the Princess Tahmina, daughter of the king of Samengān, and therefore fit to stand among the highest-born ladies in the world. Save for my father, no man has ever seen my face before this hour, nor even heard my voice. Yet for you I have taken off my veil and to you I speak boldly and without shame—and I speak in hope. Even in my seclusion I have heard the tales that are told of Rustem the tall champion, mightiest among men, who has no peer for strength and battle-craft, than whom there has never lived a better warrior. And hearing these tales, I could not but admire and love the man of whom they were told. For many years, Prince Rustem, have I been in love with you and longed and dreamt that great Ormuzd would one day send you to me, that you might become my beloved husband. Prince Rustem, I beg of you, have pity on one whose heart could easily break for love of you. Make me happy as only you can make me happy. Even should I never behold you again after this one night, yet still would I count myself the most fortunate woman in all the world. Look well at me, Prince Rustem. Am I not fair enough to be wife to the greatest warrior who has ever lived, even to you yourself?'

Amazed by her presence there and by her words, Rustem sat up and looked at her by the light of the lamp which the slave held up close beside her mistress's face. Tahmina was indeed very lovely, a bride whom any man might rejoice to have. Yet she was the daughter of an enemy, a king allied to Afrāsib, against whom Rustem had sworn to fight unceasingly, and he hesitated.

'Prince Rustem,' Tahmina whispered, 'do not condemn me to die from love of you.' She paused a moment and then went on, 'I know where your horse Raksh is hidden. Marry me, and as a bride-gift I will restore Raksh to you.'

Rustem leapt to his feet. 'This marriage,' he said, 'will it be pleasing to your father? For though he received me with friendliness today, we are enemies, he and I.'

'Leave all to me, Prince Rustem. I will persuade my father,' she said. Though Tahmina was a dutiful daughter, and though she had spoken to Rustem only the words which her father had taught her; now that she had seen and talked with him, she was far from ill-pleased by her father's choice of a husband. 'I will go to my father at this very moment, and awaken him and tell him of this matter and ask his blessing,' said Tahmina. 'By the grace of Ormuzd he will not refuse us.'

The king of Samengān, far from needing to be awakened, was waiting impatiently for his daughter's return. To have the most powerful warrior among all his enemies, bound to him by a marriage with his daughter, could not but be to his advantage. He was not foolish; he did not believe that marriage to a Turanian woman would win Rustem to the Turanian cause. But he knew that it would mean—at the least—that Rustem would spare Samengān in all his future raids over the border into Turān. He embraced Tahmina. 'You have done well, my daughter,' he said. When he thought a fitting time had passed, during which it might seem that she had been persuading him, he took her by the hand and led her back to Rustem.

'My guest and my friend,' he said, 'there is no father in all the world who could wish for a better husband for his daughter. It will be my honour and my privilege to call you my son.'

So Rustem and Tahmina were married immediately; and though the marriage was secret, with little ceremony and no wedding guests—for the king of Samengān did not mean Rustem to have time enough in which perhaps to change his mind—they were well enough pleased with each other; and in the morning Tahmina herself led Raksh to Rustem with the happy tidings that she had indeed been able to keep the promise she had made to him, and that, while they slept, Raksh had been brought to the palace.

Most joyfully Rustem and Raksh were reunited; and since Rustem had no mind to linger on Turanian soil, he soon took leave of the king. Tahmina wept a little when they parted, for it seemed hard to her to have gained as a husband the most famed warrior in the world, only to have to part from him after one day.

From his arm Rustem took off a prized amulet, a jewelled bracelet which he always wore for the sake of the good fortune which it was said to bring its wearer. This bracelet he gave to Tahmina. 'Keep this safely, fair bride,' he said. 'It is for our child, should great Ormuzd grant us one. If the child is a daughter, she may use it to bind her hair. But if we have a son, he may wear it on his arm as a charm against ill luck, even as his father has worn it for many years.' He kissed her one last time, and mounting Raksh he rode away, back to Zābulestān and safety.

They never met again. Yet in the years that followed, Tahmina thought often of her husband, and her memories of him brought her happiness. Rustem, for his part, though he never entirely forgot her, did not often remember his wife in far-away Samengān. But it pleased him when he had word from Tahmina, nine months after their parting, that they had a son. He chose three large rubies which were from among the finest in the world, and sent them to Samengān by a trusted messenger, together with three bags of gold, as a birth-gift for his son.

11: Sohrāb and Rustem

IN Samengān, Rustem's son, named Sohrāb by his mother, grew fast, and with each day that passed, his strength increased. When he was a boy of some ten years old, he was as tall and strong as any full grown man. When he looked at other boys of his own age and saw how far he surpassed them in strength and height and breadth of shoulder, he wondered at it.

One day he went to his mother Tahmina and asked her, 'Dearest mother, I easily outdo all my comrades in every game we play. Surely my father can have been no ordinary man. I beg of you, tell me who he was, that I may know how to answer anyone who asks his name.'

'My son,' Tahmina answered him, 'your father is none other than Rustem, the great Persian champion of whom all the world has heard.' And she showed him the three rubies and the three bags of gold which Rustem had sent to her at the time of Sohrāb's birth, and the amulet which he had left with her when they had parted.

Overjoyed, Sohrāb exclaimed, 'I knew in my heart that my father was a man who stood high above all other men. How proud I shall be now that, to all who ask his name of me, I can answer, "Rustem is my father".'

But Tahmina said earnestly, 'My son, the name of your father must not pass your lips. It must be a secret known only to you, to me, and to your grandfather the king. For, as you well know, your grandfather is subject to the Emperor Afrāsib and pays annual tribute to him. If Afrāsib were to learn that you are the son of the great enemy of Turān, it would go ill with us, for he would without doubt destroy you for hatred of your father. And there is yet another reason why our secret should be kept: if Rustem were to hear how fine a son he has in Samengān, he might send for you to go to him in Zābulestān, and I and your grandfather would never see you again.'

'I would not leave you yet, my mother,' said Sohrāb, 'so I shall keep silent when others ask me the name of my father—though I shall dearly wish to answer them with the proud truth.'

As all boys do, Sohrāb dreamt dreams of deeds he would one day perform. His greatest dream was of a day when he would meet with Rustem and declare himself his son and go into battle at the great warrior's side. 'One day,' he often said to Tahmina, 'I will lead an army of Turanian warriors against Persia. I will destroy Tus and Gudarz and the other Persian generals, and I will cast down the Great King Kāvus from his throne and crown my father Rustem in his stead. Then together I and my father will lead the Persian army into Turān and cast down the Emperor Afrāsib and set you as Empress in his place. Oh, my mother, if Rustem is the sun and I am the moon, when both the sun and the moon shine together in the sky, how can any lesser star still show its light?'

When Sohrāb was twelve years old, his mother found a fine horse for him, the best in all Samengān; and his grandfather the king gave him treasure and weapons and an army to lead against Persia. With his little army Sohrāb made swift raids on the Persian borderlands and came home from them with spoils to lay before his mother. But such bold doings could not remain long hidden, and they came soon to the ears of the Emperor Afrāsib, who asked questions and sent spies into Samengān, and pondered on what he learnt thereby. And finally he was convinced that this grandson of the king of Samengān could be a child of no other than great Rustem; and he determined that this son of his country's enemy should become Turān's best weapon against that enemy.

He therefore sent messages of goodwill to Sohrāb, praising him for his zeal against Persia; and he gave him a part of the imperial army to lead, and experienced generals to advise him. But to these generals he first said, in secret, 'I believe this boy to be a son of Rustem, but this must be kept from him, just as Rustem himself must not learn who Sohrāb is. One day the two will meet face to face on the battlefield, and Sohrāb, being the younger, may well destroy his father and so rid us of the greatest of those dangers which threaten our empire. Afterwards, when he has served his purpose, we may rid ourselves of Sohrāb, lest he learn of his parentage and seek to avenge his father on us.'

'But what,' Afrāsib was asked, 'if Rustem is the victor and slays Sohrāb, our young champion? What of that?'

'Why then,' smiled Afrāsib, 'we must make certain that Rustem is told who was the boy whom he slew. The knowledge should give him many a day of heartache and weaken his strength by tears. So you see, my friends, either way there is an advantage to Turān.'

And so it came that one day Sohrāb went into Persia with not only the men of Samengān, but at the head of a part of the imperial army of Turān. Happily and proudly, and ignorant of Afrāsib's twisted schemes, Sohrāb rode beside the Turanian generals as though he were already a man of twice his years, a respected warrior and the victor in many battles.

When word came to the Great King Kāvus of this invasion, he hastily sent to his generals and his champions, Giv and his father, Gudarz, Tus, and the others. And he dispatched a messenger to Rustem in Zābul—where, by Zāl's wish, Rustem now reigned, helped and advised by his father—bidding him come at once to the capital, for a young Turanian champion of terrifying might had invaded Persia with a large army. 'It is said that in strength and skill he is your equal, Rustem,' ran the message of Kāvus. 'And this may indeed be more than an idle boast made to frighten us, for I have heard it whispered that you have a son, born to you by a princess of Samengān. This youth might well be he, and if he is, then only you could be reckoned strong enough to oppose him on the field of battle.'

When Rustem had the message, he laughed. 'Kāvus is ever fearful. A dog barks and he thinks the golden tiara of the King of Kings is threatened.' He calculated the number of years since the birth of Tahmina's son. 'This youth can be no child of mine,' he said. 'My son would be too young by several years, to have achieved this young warrior's fame.' So he spoke, forgetting his own strength and skill at that age which Sohrāb had now reached. 'And if he is not my son, there can be no need to fear him, and therefore no need for haste.' And he invited his friends to a drinking-party, ignoring the command of Kāvus until such time as it pleased him to present himself at court.

By then Kāvus was very much afraid, and fear had made him angry. Stupid, as he had ever been, he railed furiously at his mightiest and most valued champion, Persia's best hope of victory, calling him traitor and coward, and swearing that if he had a sword in his hand at that moment, he would himself strike off Rustem's head. When he ceased his shouting for lack of breath, he could only gesture towards Rustem and bid his guards, in a whisper, 'Take this wretch and hang him on a high gallows. I allow no man to flout my commands.'

No one was foolhardy enough to obey so outrageous an order, and no guard stirred. Regaining his breath, Kāvus addressed Giv, the son of his general Gudarz. 'Do you take and hang him, Giv, if you have any loyalty to me.'

Giv protested, and at once Kāvus was as angry with him as he was with Rustem. 'Take them and hang them both,' he commanded Tus, another of the generals.

Reluctantly Tus went to Rustem and took him by the arm to lead him away.

At this Rustem lost his temper and spoke as no one else would have dared to speak to the Great King, and King of Kings. 'Must you always be so foolish, so unfitted for your high office as the ruler of Persia's great empire?' he asked Kāvus. 'Save your gallows for the Turanians. Do not cut down those who hold up your throne, lest it topple and take you with it. It is through me and through Gudarz and Giv and those like us, that you keep your mighty state. Are you mad, to destroy yourself by destroying us? Away with your gallows! I am returning to Zābulestān. You can fight your own war with Turān.'

Kāvus grew calmer; and after both he and Rustem had been urged by the others to forsake their threats, they were persuaded to friendliness once more; and Rustem agreed to ride with the generals and the imperial army and help drive back the Turanian invaders.

Not many days had passed before the two armies met and fell to the attack. Among the Turanians, Sohrāb acquitted himself as bravely as his mother had known he would; but while he fought, he was ever searching keenly about the battlefield for a sight of Rustem. Now and then he glimpsed among the Persians a tall warrior mounted upon a golden-yellow, red-dappled horse; and each time he saw him, laying about him with his huge sword and slaying with each stroke, he eagerly asked, 'Is that great Rustem?' But no one answered 'Yes.' Some because they had never before seen Rustem and so therefore could not name him, and the others because Afrāsib had bidden them keep the truth from Sohrāb.

At the end of the first day's fighting, men had died on either side, but neither army had gained the advantage. A certain Persian warrior had been captured alive, and Sohrāb hopefully questioned him. 'Is Rustem, king of Zābulestān, the great champion of Persia, come to war?'

Seeing Sohrāb's great height and the strong muscles of his arms and thighs, from which he had put off his armour, the Persian warrior was fearful that here, at last, might be a Turanian champion who would prove a match for Rustem. Afraid for the Persian cause he sought to protect Rustem. He shook his head and lied. 'No, Rustem is not with us in the camp. Nor is he likely to join with us.' Then in his heart he blessed the impulse which had made him hide the truth, when he saw—saw and misunderstood—the instant downward droop of Sohrāb's mouth and how the light went out in his eager eyes.

Because he had believed the captive's words, the next day, early in the fighting, when Sohrāb saw with admiration, battling close beside him, the tall warrior on the yellow-gold horse, he did not ask if it were Rustem who was striking down right and left of him as he cleft a path for himself through the Turanian ranks. Instead Sohrāb cried out to the Persian, challenging him to single combat; and Rustem, laughing and pleased—for he had noted and approved the courage and skill of this young, unknown Turanian champion—accepted the challenge. The two armies ceased their struggle and drew away from each other, and warriors rested while they watched the battle between these two adversaries, both far taller and stronger than the common run of men.

Rustem, confident as always, had expected to overcome the young Turanian with customary ease; and he was astonished to find his opponent well matched to him, not only in stature, but in strength and skill also; and he thought to himself, 'Never have I striven with one whose strength and craft so nearly equal mine. Were it not that this young man seems twice his age, I would say that here was my own son. In time, when he has seen twice the years he has already lived, Tahmina's child will be such a warrior as this, and it will be a proud day when I meet with him and acknowledge him my son.'

When evening fell and their combat ceased, both Rustem and Sohrāb were weary and bruised, and bleeding from a score of petty wounds. And each felt for the other a respect and a strange liking. As, with warriors' formal courtesy, they parted, Sohrāb stared hard at Rustem, frowning a little in perplexity. Boyishly impetuous, he asked, 'I have heard that Rustem, king of Zābulestān, is not with the Persian army. Yet surely you must be Rustem and no other?'

But Rustem was suddenly ashamed that, in this unknown young Turanian champion, he had found one of equal skill at arms, and on an impulse he said, 'You were told truly. Rustem is not here.'

In the Turanian camp that evening, the champions and generals rested, feasting while the musicians played and sang to them. But Sohrāb was silent and thoughtful and could not cast out from his mind the thought of the man with whom he had fought that day. At last he turned to Humān, brother of the much-respected general Pirān, and said, 'You saw that Persian champion with whom I strove today. You have surely seen Rustem in former battles. Was this man not Rustem? And his yellow horse, it seemed to me to be most like Raksh, as I have heard him described.'

Humān, obedient to the command of Afrāsib, answered, 'I have seen Rustem often in the past, and I have myself fought against him —and been fortunate to escape with my life. That champion whom you challenged was not Rustem, nor was his horse Raksh.'

And Sohrāb believed him, for he knew of no reason why Humān should lie to him. Yet he could not entirely rid his mind of its doubts and his heart of its strange liking for his adversary; and when, the next morning, they met once again, rested and armed and once more ready and eager, Sohrāb smiled at Rustem as though they were old friends whose previous parting had been after an evening of drinking and converse, and not on a battlefield. He said, 'Champion of Persia, let others fight this war, but let us two make peace together. What say you, shall we cast down our weapons and eat and drink and talk together, forgetting Afrāsib and Kāvus and their quarrels?'

But though Rustem felt for the youth a liking equal to his own, he replied, 'Your mood changes very swiftly, young man. Yesterday you were all for fighting, yet today you speak of wine and feasting.' He laughed. 'Much as I care for food and drink, you will not win me to you by such means. You serve Afrāsib and I serve Kāvus. We are enemies and must so remain. Come, let us waste no more time on words. I am already tired of this war. I would see it over and Kāvus victorious, that I may the sooner return to my own home.'

'And is that home not Zābulestān, and are you not Rustem, son of Zāl?' Sohrāb asked for the last time.

'Come, why all this talk and these questions—unless you have lost your courage and fear me?' exclaimed Rustem, adding, 'But courage, I think, you are not one to lose, so let us fight, and Ormuzd will protect that one of us whom he wishes to preserve, and allow the other to die.'

By consent of both, being so well matched in stature, they dismounted at the very outset of their meeting, laid aside their weapons and fell to wrestling instead. They struggled and twisted, the advantage first with one and then with the other; but neither of them was able to throw the other to the ground. At last, after several hours, when both were weary yet still eager, a swift move on Sohrāb's part, made with all his strength, caused Rustem to slip and fall. Instantly, before he could rise, Sohrāb was upon him and drawing his dagger, ready to cut Rustem's throat.

Rustem put up his hand and grasped Sohrāb's wrist. 'Not so fast, my friend. In Persia it is not our custom to slay an opponent at the first fall. We allow him to rise and wrestle again. It is only at the second fall that we count ourselves as victors and dispatch the loser with our sharp blades.'

Sohrāb hesitated. Then he said, 'Since we are fighting upon Persian soil, let us keep to Persian custom.' And he sheathed his dagger and rose, allowing Rustem to do likewise. Then they parted for that day, and each returned to his comrades to rest and refresh himself for a further day's combat in the morning.

Humān, who had watched him all day, said to Sohrāb, 'What folly came into your mind today, that you set free the lion you had trapped, and spared the life of an enemy—and that enemy one so strong and dangerous to Turān? Truly, you have wasted all for which you have striven so many toilsome, painful hours, and are like to lose your life from it.'

'Never fear,' Sohrāb answered confidently, 'tomorrow he dies, while I shall be victorious. I shall live to hear you praise me for my victory, Humān.'

But Rustem, once the fighting was over and done for that day, went to a fresh, clear-flowing spring and drank from it. Then, when he had washed himself from the stains of battle in the cool water, he prayed. 'Great Ormuzd, tomorrow give me the victory over this Turanian youth, that I am not shamed for ever in the sight of men, by being worsted by a young and unknown boy.' And Rustem's prayer was heard and answered, to his own undoing and great sorrow.

The next morning when they met again, Rustem came to the place of their meeting heavy-hearted and disinclined towards both defeat and victory. He feared the shame of defeat at the hands of a young and nameless adversary; and though he wished for victory, yet he had a strange reluctance to kill so brave and skilled a youth. But Sohrāb came to the place of meeting filled with confidence and with the determination to finish their combat that very day and be victorious over the older, more experienced man. It would, he thought—his father Rustem never being far from his mind in these days of battle—be a fine deed of which to tell him when at last they met. He was eager to have done with the deed, but only that he might boast of it to his father and win his approval: he had no hatred for the man with whom he had striven throughout two long days, and felt only admiration and respect for him.

That morning they fought on horseback until the fine edges of their swords were blunted; then they dismounted and fought on foot, dagger against dagger, each circling the other warily, seeking for the opening which would give him the chance of a blow that would end their combat. And then to Rustem it came, that instant of dropped guard; and in that same instant Rustem's dagger had flashed in and up and down, and was buried to the hilt in Sohrāb's breast. With a heavy sigh, Sohrāb sank to the ground. His eyes looked up, straight into Rustem's eyes; and Rustem knelt beside him and, with a gentleness he could not have explained, drew out the dagger, and the blood streamed after the reddened blade.

'A cruel fate,' said Sohrāb, 'to die before I reach full manhood and achieve all I promised to achieve. Yet I brought it on myself. Had I not been so eager to find my father and to have some great deed of which to boast to him, I would not now be dying.' A sob shook him. 'Oh, that I had lived to see him—even once, only once—before I died.' He was silent for a moment, his eyes closed. When he opened them again it was to say, 'I shall never now see my father's face, nor will he ever look on mine. Yet, when he hears men speak of this day's work, he will be swift to avenge me. O champion of Persia, beware of a champion greater than yourself. Beware of Rustem, the greatest of all, for when he learns of the death of Sohrāb his son, he will not let it pass unavenged. Though you were to become a fish among the million fish of the ocean, or a star among the million stars of the sky; if you were to put out the light of the sun that you might hide yourself in everlasting night, Rustem would still hunt you down and find you. If I have but a few seconds more to live, you have days to the same number.'

The shock of the truth struck Rustem like a blow upon his heart. He gasped and his mind reeled from it. Yet, now that he knew the truth, he knew also that he had known it, without recognizing it, all the time. 'What token have you, that you are Rustem's son?' he asked, though he knew that he already had all the proof he needed; it was in the sight of the tall, straight body, the strong arms, the battle-skill and courage of the boy—and in the ache of his own heart.

'Oh, it is the truth. It is no brag. The dying have no need to boast. You will find the token on my arm, where my mother Tahmina fastened it: Rustem's bracelet which he gave her when they parted. She said it would be an amulet to keep me safe in battle, as well as a token to my father, when I met with him. But now I shall never find

him, though it was only to seek him, and not to fight for Afrāsib, that I rode out to this war.'

For a while Rustem could not speak, and then he said, 'You have found him, Sohrāb. I am Rustem.'

They looked for a long moment into each other's eyes. 'It is an unkindly deed, for a father to slay his own son,' said Sohrāb. 'Yet

I brought it on myself. Even when you denied the truth, I should have believed my heart.'

With his large hands moving more gently than they had ever moved before, Rustem took off Sohrāb's armour to ease him, laying aside the silver-decorated helmet and the jacket plated with bronze. With his fingers pressing on the wound to stop its bleeding, he sat upon the ground with Sohrāb laid across his knees and encircled by his arms. And so they remained, while time passed and the sun dropped to its setting.

Several of Rustem's men came to him. He looked at them as if he did not know them and only said, 'I have slain my son.' At first, when they questioned him further, he did not seem to understand their questions; then, while very slowly recognition and understanding returned to his glance, he still repeated only, 'I have slain my son.'

By then word of what had befallen had reached to the other champions and the generals of Persia, and with eyes which no longer saw nothing of the things at which they looked, Rustem was aware of Gudarz standing close by him.

'Gudarz, my friend, I have heard it said that the Great King has ward of a magical draught for the healing of wounds and all ills, a divine gift to the world from Ormuzd. Ride swiftly to him, Gudarz, and ask him—if he remembers the deeds I have done for him and for Persia—to send me a drop. It may be that by its means my son will live.'

Gudarz went, riding as swiftly as any man might. But when, travel-worn and weary, he stood before the Great King and repeated Rustem's words, Kāvus, always stupid, hesitated, thinking, 'Rustem has indeed done much for me. If this son of his lives to be such another as his father, then might I have two Rustems to do great deeds for me. Yet Rustem is free and independent in spirit, he is not to be lightly commanded here and there. This son of his may well resemble him in this, and together the two of them might one day defy me and afflict me more than all the champions and warriors of Turān together.' And he refused Rustem's request and would not send the draught which might have saved Sohrāb's life.

Gudarz was angry and spoke bitterly to Kāvus. Then, waiting for no reply to his words, he rode away, back to the Persian camp.

Rustem did not know how long—minutes, hours, or days—he had been sitting on the ground with Sohrāb in his arms, before he heard a voice above him and looked up to see Gudarz there.

'The Great King is stony-hearted and a fool. He will not send the magical draught,' said Gudarz. 'Yet if you were to go to him yourself and ask it, Rustem, he might be moved and persuaded.'

'I will go,' said Rustem. He laid Sohrāb gently down upon a bed of cloaks and pillows that had been brought from his pavilion, and with a last look at his son's pale face, he rose and went to mount Raksh while Gudarz held the bridle. But he was hardly in the saddle when he heard his name called and saw a man come running from the place where Sohrāb lay. He did not even need to hear the words which the man spoke, he knew them before they were uttered.

'Lord, your son is dead.'

Rustem, on Raksh, bowed his head and wept.

12: Siyāvush the Unfortunate

ONE day three of the courtiers of the Great King Kāvus, the two generals Tus and Gudarz, and Giv, who was the son of Gudarz, rode out hunting in the forest near the Turanian border with a cheerful company of followers. In their pursuit of game, Tus and young Giv galloped faster than their companions and had soon outstripped the others. But they reined in their horses and stared in surprise when they beheld, right in their path, a fair young maiden, the fairest they had ever seen. She was clad in rich garments of fine embroidered cloth, fastened with a set of golden pins whose heads were the heads of beasts, carved in lapis lazuli. Crystal ear-rings hung from her ears and crystal sparkled in her hair; and about her slender throat glowed jasper and cornelians. For a moment they were too astonished at seeing her there, alone and so beautiful, to have any words to say; then Tus, the elder by several years, recovering his wits first, spoke to her and asked her who she was. She told them that she was a high-born Turanian lady, a kinswoman of Garsivāz, brother to the Emperor Afrāsib; and that she had fled to the forest from the cruelty of her father.

She was so lovely that both the men wished to have her for a wife. 'I saw her first,' said Giv. 'She should be mine.'

'I spoke to her first,' retorted Tus. 'She is mine.'

In no time at all they were quarrelling bitterly over her; and soon each had reached a point at which he was ready to strike her lovely head from her body, sooner than give her up to his friend.

Fortunately, by this time certain of their companions had caught up with them; and one man now intervened and said, 'My friends, this is unworthy of you. Cease your quarrelling and take the maiden to the Great King. Let him make the decision between you.'

This advice seeming good to them, they did as he suggested and escorted the maiden to the imperial palace and laid the matter before the Great King, and King of Kings, for his judgement.

Kāvus gave one long look at the maiden and smiled to himself as he listened to the protests of Tus and Giv. When they were done, he said, 'Truly, your hunting this day has brought in the fairest of all game. It is as though two lions had outrun and caught the sun. But perhaps it were best that the choice lay with the maiden.' And he asked her, 'Fairest of women, what is your rank and birth?'

'My mother is a princess, kinswoman to Prince Garsivāz of Turān. My father is of the line of Feridun, who was your own ancestor, Great King.'

'One so nobly born and of such rare beauty deserves only the highest and the best. Even the King of Kings himself would not disdain to call you his wife.' He smiled at her and she understood his meaning. 'Fair lady,' he bade her, 'say now whose wife you would be.'

'Great King,' she answered, 'out of all men in the world, there is only the one whose wife I would willingly call myself. That man is you.'

Kāvus, usually so stupid, was delighted by his own unwonted cunning. He smiled at his two dismayed and outwitted courtiers. 'She has chosen,' he said. 'So be it.'

In this manner a Turanian noblewoman became one of the wives of the Great King Kāvus; and in time a son was born to them, a boy with all his mother's rare beauty, whom Kāvus named Siyāvush. As soon as Siyāvush was old enough to learn the arts of war, Kāvus sent him to Zābul and gave him into the protection of Rustem, whom he considered the most fitted in all Persia to teach the boy skill of arms, horsemanship, and that love of truth and justice that were the birthright of a prince; and Siyāvush soon proved himself the best of pupils.

One so beautiful, so accomplished and so honourable, deserved only happiness from life; yet Siyāvush had little but ill fortune from the day he left Rustem's care and returned to his father's palace in the capital, to take his allotted place in the life of the court, a youth of great charm who was soon liked by all men, rich and poor. The first of his misfortunes was the most grievous of them, the one from which all the others were to spring; and which was, in the end, to cost him his life. Sudāba, his father's lovely young queen, immediately she saw him, fancied herself in love with the handsome youth. She lost no time in sending for him to tell him of her feelings. Siyāvush, reared by Rustem to respect honour above all else, was appalled by her treachery to his father, and did not hide from her his contempt and scorn. Sudāba was a spiteful and wicked woman, and at once abandoning all her supposed love for Siyāvush, she went to Kāvus to complain of him with many tears and much wringing of her hands, imputing to Siyāvush all her own evil thoughts and desires. She told Kāvus that Siyāvush was an unworthy son, treacherous to his father and guilty of foul cruelty and violence to his father's queen.

When Kāvus sent for Siyāvush and bade him answer his step-mother's accusations, Siyāvush denied all guilt and, in his turn, accused Sudāba. Kāvus held both his queen and his son in affection, and he could not make up his mind as to which of them was lying. Whichever was, for the moment, with him and speaking to him, seemed to be telling the truth. First he would believe the one, casting the other from his favour; and then, after a few days had passed, swayed by further denials or accusations, he would decide that he had been mistaken and bestow his favour again upon that one of the two whom he had previously rejected.

And so matters went for several months, to the great unhappiness of the innocent Siyāvush; until such time as the queen's accusations became so outrageous that even the stupid Kāvus hesitated to believe them.

'Let them both undergo the ordeal,' he said. 'Let the divine fire of Ormuzd decide between them.' And he ordered a huge pyre to be built of great quantities of wood overlaid with pitch. When a torch was set to this pyre it blazed up instantly; the flames rose high and all who stood near by shrank back from the great heat, as though from a white-hot furnace. Kāvus sent for Siyāvush and Sudāba and bade them make ready to pass through the fire. 'This way,' he said, 'will great Ormuzd display the truth to me and to all men, and the matter between my queen and my son shall be settled once and for ever. By the grace of Ormuzd, that one of you who is innocent of wrongdoing shall pass through the fire unscathed, while the guilty one shall burn.'

Sudāba, terrified, hid her fear as well as she might, upbraiding Kāvus, with a great show of injured virtue and indignation, for his doubts and his cruelty; and she refused to undergo the ordeal. Siyāvush, on the other hand, eagerly declared himself ready to endure any ordeal, so only that he might prove his innocence to his father and to the world. Clad all in white, he knelt before Kāvus and said, 'I thank you that you have allowed me thus to show my loyalty and love for you, lord father. Have no fear for me, for I am innocent and great Ormuzd will keep me safe from all harm.' He sent for his favourite black horse and mounted. Then, spurring on the brave beast, he rode into the fire and was lost to sight behind the tall, roaring flames.

Everyone there waited anxiously and some began to weep, for young Siyāvush was still as much loved as he had ever been. The guilty queen stood, stiff and tense, staring, staring into the dazzling

blaze of the pyre, not even daring to hope that Ahrimān might come to the aid of one who followed the way of deceit and falsehood and, therefore, might suppose herself dear to him.

And then, beyond the flames and the smoke, at the farther side of the pyre, Siyāvush appeared and a great sigh went up from all the people. He was unharmed, and his black horse also; not even his white garments were scorched. He dismounted and ran to his father, who embraced him with tears of joy; and the people, flinging off their apprehension, cheered and cried aloud in praise of their beloved young prince.

At that moment, in the anger which he felt against his faithless queen, Kāvus would have had Sudāba put to death; but generously Siyāvush pleaded for her, so Kāvus spared her life. But he cast her off, to be called his wife no longer. After that, Kāvus heaped great honours upon Siyāvush and proclaimed him his heir. But, complacent and obstinate, before more than a very few years had passed, he restored rank and favour to Sudāba, thereby appearing to discredit Siyāvush once again.

At this time, in Turān, the Emperor Afrāsib was gradually gathering together his forces and making ready for an attack upon Persia. The Great King Kāvus ignored the rumours which reached him of these preparations for war, and he gave no heed to the advice of his counsellors. Afrāsib, his preparations completed, led a hundred thousand horsemen over the River Oxus into Persia. When word of this was brought to Kāvus he was in the women's apartments of his palace, drinking and making merry. The shock of this surprise—which should have been no surprise to him—almost took from him what little sense he possessed. Hastily he gave orders for his army to be called together while he summoned his counsellors to him.

'These tidings are grievous,' he said. 'Yet do not despair, for I myself shall lead the warriors of Persia against our enemies.'

His counsellors ventured to remind him of his disastrous attack upon Māzendarān and its consequences, and suggested that he would do better to appoint an experienced warrior as commander of his army, and leave the conduct of the war in abler hands.

'It is I, the Great King, and King of Kings, who must lead the men of Persia,' Kāvus insisted. 'There is no one more fitted for so responsible a task.'

'There is brave Gudarz, and there is Tus, and your many other generals beside. There is even Rustem, if he could be prevailed upon to take command. Have you forgotten all these, Great King? Who could be abler than your generals and your champions for this enterprise?'

'Gudarz, Tus, Rustem, and the others? They are all good warriors, you speak truly,' said Kāvus. 'But the men of Persia should be led into battle in this grave moment of their history by one of royal blood. I, the Great King, and King of Kings, and not Tus or Gudarz or Rustem, shall ride before them against Afrāsib.'

But Siyāvush, who had been restless and unhappy since his stepmother had regained her place as queen, thought he saw in this invasion of the land an opportunity to be free, for a time, at least, from both his father's changeable affections and his own uncomfortable knowledge that in the women's quarters Sudāba was smiling slyly and maliciously in her final triumph over him. He went to Kāvus.

'I am of royal blood, my father,' he said. 'Give me leave to lead the imperial army against our enemies.'

Kāvus, by now at heart not sorry to be spared the duty he had so rashly laid upon himself, granted Siyāvush his permission and gave the army into his charge, insisting only that Rustem, as an experienced warrior, should go with him as protector and lieutenant.

Rustem was sent for, and came, this time, with all speed from Zābulestān; the Banner of Kāva was raised and, with Siyāvush and Rustem riding before them under the bright, fluttering Banner, the men of Persia set out once again to protect their empire from the Turanian invaders.

13: Afrāsib

In his magnificent pavilion, in the midst of the camping-ground of his great army, on a couch of cushions, lay Afrāsib, Emperor of Turān. He had been strangely uneasy all the day, as though his life were nearing some great climax, or as though some inevitable and calamitous happening were fast drawing near; and now he tossed in a restless sleep. He began to dream, and his dream was most terrible, unlike any dream that had afflicted him before. In this nightmare Afrāsib found himself standing before his strongly guarded pavilion on the edge of a wide, drear desert. As far as he could see, the desert stretched before him to the horizon; and on the sands of this desert writhed and twisted a million snakes. Their hissing rose to the very sky; and as he looked upwards he saw that that sky was darkened by the wings of countless eagles whose harsh cries mingled with the hissing of the snakes. Afrāsib turned for comfort to the tall guards who kept watch about his pavilion, but he gained no solace from the sight of them, for, beyond the guards, approaching at great speed, there was a black and mighty cloud of dust. Swiftly this cloud came ever nearer; and in the wind of its coming Afrāsib's imperial banner that stood above his pavilion streamed out, tugging at the post from which it flew, as though it would have fled in fear before the oncoming cloud.

When the cloud was close enough, Afrāsib could see that it was a vast army of the horsemen of Persia, dark and menacing. Each man in this army carried a spear, and on the top of every spear grinned a whitened skull. A second skull was held in the crook of each rider's arm. This black army passed over Afrāsib's pavilion, leaving it crushed to the ground with, around it, the headless bodies of his guards. The great, grim multitude galloped relentlessly on towards Afrāsib himself; and so it passed over him, while he felt himself, with hands bound and helpless, trampled beneath the hooves of the black horses of Persia. When all the army had passed over him, he found himself in the midst of a band of horsemen, taller and fiercer even than the others, who snatched him up in their strong hands and, raising him aloft, high above their black helmets, bore him, utterly alone and without a single man of his own—friend, or follower, or kinsman—to defend him, into the presence of the Great King Kāvus. Kāvus was sitting upon a throne so high that it

touched the clouds; and beside Kāvus, on another towering throne, there sat a youth of great beauty. Afrāsib felt himself flung to the ground before these thrones and he heard the youth give a cry of triumph and saw him draw his sword. From his high throne the young man leant down and with one sweep of his impossibly far-reaching arm, he cut Afrāsib's body in two. With the pain and terror of the blow, Afrāsib cried aloud and was awakened by his own cries to find himself safe in his pavilion, with his whole army encamped around him.

His bodyguard came running to his side. 'What ails you, lord Emperor, that you cried out thus?' they asked him, much perturbed. But Afrāsib lay weeping with the terror of his nightmare and could not answer them. Greatly distressed, the guards sent word to the pavilion of Garsivāz, Afrāsib's brother; and he came hastily through a camp which was now disturbed and apprehensive, fearing some terrible mishap to the Emperor.

Garsivāz, calling for more lights to be brought, flung his arms about Afrāsib; but Afrāsib cowered away from him. 'It is I, my brother. Do not turn from me,' said Garsivāz. 'What is amiss? Are you sick? Tell me, that I may serve you as best I can.'

But Afrāsib, though soon a little reassured by the presence of his brother, could only groan and tremble. 'Do not question me, but keep your arms about me, dear brother,' he whispered at last, 'for I have had a fearful dream.' After a while, when he grew calmer, he told all his nightmare to Garsivāz. When he had ended, he said, 'By the grace of Ormuzd may no other man ever dream a dream such as mine, and suffer as I have suffered this night.'

Garsivāz, seeking to comfort his brother, said, 'Dreams are not always what they seem. Often do they portend the contrary of that of which they appear to warn us. Send for the interpreters of dreams, Afrāsib my brother, for they may bring you reassurance.'

Afrāsib did so; and with the dawn came the wise men of Turān to his pavilion, the seers and the wonder-workers and the astrologers; and to them Afrāsib told his dream. When he had done, they sat silent, and the chief among them covered his eyes with his hands and looked into the future. After a time he spoke. 'I see an army, a mighty army of the men of Persia approaching. The men in this army are angry, and they bring death to you, O emperor, even as you saw it in your dream.' The seer opened his eyes and bowed his head to the ground. 'Do not blame me, lord Emperor, for I have but spoken the truth as I saw it.'

Afrāsib and Garsivāz grew pale. 'Is there any way by which my death may be averted?' asked Afrāsib.

The seer closed his eyes and once more saw into his mind. Then he said, 'Give up this war against Persia. Send hostages and messengers with gifts to Siyāvush and Rustem, who lead the army of the Great King Kāvus, and beg that they will carry your words to Kāvus and ask for peace and a treaty of friendship. This way alone may you avert destruction.'

So Afrāsib sent messengers bearing rich gifts of gold and silver, bronze and iron, to the Persian army, with messages of goodwill, asking for peace; and hostages to show his sincerity.

Though he had no fear of death in battle, and no fear at all of fighting, Siyāvush was pleased by Afrāsib's messages and gifts, and glad that he had sent hostages unasked. 'It is well,' he said to Rustem, 'that there should be peace between the two great empires of Persia and Turān. Let us hold back from battle for now, while word is carried to my father that Afrāsib sues for peace.'

Rustem, never one to trust a Turanian promise, and always ready for a battle against his country's enemies, spoke against the counsel of Siyāvush and was all for returning the gifts and the hostages immediately, and then marching on and attacking the Turanian camp with no delay. But Siyāvush was the Great King's son and his heir, and Rustem had to give way in the matter. So Siyāvush sent Rustem to Kāvus with Afrāsib's offers of peace, while he himself remained with the army, encamped and idle.

Kāvus sat upon his golden throne, a carven lion—the beast of kings—on either side of him; and on the wall behind his head a carven frieze showing the Great King, and King of Kings, leading his army, and hunting, and slaying a bull—the beast of sacrifice—and receiving the homage of his subject-rulers; and always above the Great King's figure, hovered the winged disc of Ormuzd the divine. Kāvus sat upon his throne beneath the symbol of Ormuzd the pure and the good and he heard all that Rustem had to tell him; then he said excitedly, 'For some reason Afrāsib has of a sudden become afraid of us. He sends messages of goodwill and sues for peace with gifts and hostages, and he doubtless expects us to accept them and make an end of this war which he himself began. We now have him at a disadvantage and we would be foolish not to act swiftly. Go back to my son Siyāvush and bid him make a great fire and cast into it all the gifts of Afrāsib. Tell him to slay every one of the hostages and, before Afrāsib has time to learn of his intent, to fall upon the Turanian camp and put it to fire and sword. That shall be my answer to Afrāsib's messages.'

Though ready for fighting as he ever was, and though, as always, eager to destroy the might of Turān, yet Rustem was outraged by the commands of Kāvus. 'To act thus, to slay hostages without a cause, and to attack under the armour of peace while the present truce still lasts, would be to act as cowards and contemptibly, and could do our fame no good.'

Kāvus grew angry and demanded that Rustem should do as he ordered. But still Rustem refused. The more angry Kāvus grew, the more stubborn Rustem became; until at last Kāvus not only ordered him from his presence and from the city, but forbade him to return to his own kingdom of Zābulestān; and even, in his thoughtless rage, exiled his greatest champion to a far distant province, to leave there on pain of death. Then he sent word to Siyāvush, ordering him to slaughter the hostages and to lead an attack on Afrāsib by stealth, before the truce was ended.

Siyāvush was dismayed by this false dealing of his father, and appalled to learn what had befallen the honest Rustem, whose only offence had been to desire to act according to the rules of honourable warfare, and to save his sovereign from the scorn and contempt which his shameful deeds would win him. After Siyāvush had thought long and deeply on the matter, he decided to disobey the Great King, because it seemed to him the only upright and proper course, and because peace ever brings less suffering to men than war. He ordered the Persian army back to the capital and freed the Turanian hostages. And then—not because he feared the certain anger of his father, but because he could no longer admire and respect one who would so lightly have broken a truce and murdered hostages—Siyāvush, alone, went to the Turanian camp. There, he offered Afrāsib his friendship and asked leave to dwell peaceably somewhere on Turanian soil.

Afrāsib, overjoyed that he had successfully averted the fearful fate threatened in his dream, welcomed Siyāvush, giving him gifts and a fine palace to live in; and, moreover, he bestowed on him his own daughter, Farangis, as a wife. Garsivāz, too, at first embraced the son of his kinswoman and showed Siyāvush much kindness.

So young Siyāvush married Farangis and dwelt in great honour among the Turanians for a year or two. But Siyāvush had been ill-fated from his birth and he was not destined for a life that was either long or happy. Too soon his kinsman Garsivāz grew envious of the favour shown to him by Afrāsib, fearing that in time Siyāvush might take the place that he himself had always held in his brother's affection. The more regard Afrāsib showed to Siyāvush, the deeper and crueller grew the jealousy of Garsivāz; and as the days passed, little by little he began to slander Siyāvush to Afrāsib, until he saw Afrāsib's affection for the young man turn first to fear and then to hatred. And so at last, through this fear, Afrāsib most shamefully had Siyāvush put to death.

Garsivāz would have wished Farangis, also, slain; but before Afrāsib could be persuaded, most unnaturally, to kill his own innocent daughter, the noble-hearted general Pirān, now commander of the whole Turanian imperial army, swiftly and secretly took her to his palace in his own kingdom of Khotān, where she remained hidden in the apartments of Pirān's daughters, sorrowing bitterly for the loss of her young husband. And there in Khotān, a month or two later, the son of Siyāvush was born, and Farangis wept anew that his father had never lived to see their child, whom she named Khosroes.

It seemed an ill thing to Pirān that the child's grandfather should not know of his birth; also, he feared that jealous Garsivāz, who still hunted Farangis, might in time come to discover where she was hidden and learn, also, of the birth of Khosroes and bring harm to mother and child. Therefore, after careful debate with himself on the matter, a few months after the birth of Khosroes he sought private audience with Afrāsib.

When the two men were alone together, Pirān knelt before his Emperor. 'Great lord of Turān,' he said, 'it is my duty to make known to you the birth of one who is the most humble and inconsiderable of all your subjects. So meek and poor he is, and so much without pretence to rank, and so much lacking all ambitious thoughts, that he might well be called the most lowly of your slaves. Yet he is beautiful, lord Emperor, and for that reason alone it seemed to me fitting that you should hear of his birth. Humble and obscure he may be, yet in looks he is your great ancestor Feridun reborn. Slave he may be considered, yet in appearance and promise he would not be unworthy to be called your grandson.'

Afrāsib understood Pirān's meaning. For a while he was silent and thoughtful; then he answered with a sigh, 'Sometimes of late I have regretted the death of Siyāvush. He was brave and noble and much loved of my daughter, and perhaps it was not all true, that which I came to believe of him.' He fell into silence again for another moment or so and then said at last, 'When I was a boy, my tutor told me once of an old prophecy that a time would come when a great hero, born of the imperial lines of both Turān and Persia, should rule those two empires so wisely and justly that all men would bless his name and offer thanks to great Ormuzd that they had the fair fortune to live during his reign. Perchance this child of whom you have today told me, is that hero of whom my tutor spoke. If this be so indeed, then he must grow up in safety, free from the malice of my brother Garsivāz. Yet, for the sake of the love I bear my brother, I will not take upon myself the task of rearing and protecting him. So do you, Pirān, carry the child to the mountains. There let him be cared for by the simple shepherds who pasture their flocks on the foot-hills. He shall grow up among them, knowing the name of neither his father nor his mother. If he is indeed destined for great glory, fate itself will bring him to his rightful place when the time is ripe. As for his mother, my daughter Farangis, let her return in safety to the palace I gave to Siyāvush, and dwell there with all honour, as is fitting for the daughter of an emperor.' So Afrāsib spoke, treading a narrow path between his conscience and his affection for his daughter on the one hand, and, on the other, his love for his brother and his fears of one day losing his throne to this son of Siyāvush.

Pirān had not gained all that he wanted—Afrāsib's open acceptance of Khosroes as his grandson and his naming of him as his heir—but he had made certain that, little good as he was willing to do for him, neither would Afrāsib, for a time at least, do the child any harm.

14: Khosroes and Afrāsib

MANY months passed before word of the secret death of Siyāvush came to Persia to be received with great sorrow by the people who had so much loved him. In the palace of the Great King, Queen Sudāba alone laughed for joy that in the end it was she who had triumphed and survived her enemy. Kāvus was divided in his feelings at the tidings, unsure of whether to weep for his once-loved son, or to reflect with satisfaction that, for his disobedience and his defiance, he had deserved no better fate. His mood changed hourly; in turn, for many days, he shed tears at one moment and at the next exclaimed, 'So perish all who defy me and rebel against my commands.'

News from the other regions of the wide empire of Persia only crawled lamely to that distant province to which Rustem had been banished; and when at last he heard of the death of his foster-child and pupil, several years had passed and Khosroes, among the shepherds in Turān, had already grown to a handsome boy. Rustem was so angered by the murder that, caring nothing for the sentence of the Great King, he came storming back from exile, vowing vengeance on all who were to blame for the fate of Siyāvush. Kāvus was not entirely sorry to see his tall champion once again, even though Rustem's vengeance began immediately and very close to the imperial throne.

'All the ill that befell Siyāvush had its birth with the queen,' Rustem exclaimed; and sword in hand he forced his way into the women's quarters of the palace, even to the very apartments of the queen herself. There he seized Sudāba by her long black hair, dragged her from the protection of her servants and, in spite of her screams and the protests of her women, he slew her; and so his vengeance for Siyāvush was well begun.

In Turān kindly Pirān secretly kept a protecting eye upon young Khosroes, visiting him from time to time in the guise of a poor traveller or a passing herdsman, as he grew to a tall, strong boy among the shepherds, herding their flocks with them, dressed in rough skins and barefoot, sharing the plain fare on which they lived and appearing to all who knew him, to be of no more consequence than any of his simple fosterers. But Pirān had seen to it that Khosroes knew—and kept to himself—the secret of his birth; and he ever hoped that one day the boy would succeed to the throne of his grandfather Afrāsib. Then there came a day when this seemed no more unlikely than that the boy would grow up to be a shepherd, or indeed, to grown up at all.

Throughout the years since the Emperor Afrāsib had sent Khosroes to dwell among poor shepherds, he had thought often of the boy, and he had had time enough in which to wonder whether he had been wise to spare his life—perhaps thereby shortening his own. For, in the space of that one night when, encamped on Persian soil amid his army, he had dreamt his fearful dream, Afrāsib—that one-time fighting-man and crafty general—had lost all his warrior's skill and all his courage, and had become an ageing, fearful man, ever given to brooding and often assailed by nightmares. And now, the more he thought on the matter of Khosroes, the more unwise his conduct appeared to him; and at last he sent for Pirān.

'It is about the son of Siyāvush that I would speak with you,' he said when Pirān had entered his presence and all others been dismissed. 'I have thought long and carefully on the matter and I am now convinced that I acted rashly in sparing his life. My days are made a torment and my nights are sleepless because of this boy. He must die, as did his father, before he becomes a danger to me and to all Turān. See to this for me, my good and loyal Pirān.'

Pirān's first dismayed response to these words would have been to exclaim in protestation against so cruel a demand, but he checked himself in time and said, 'Let it be as you command, lord Emperor. Yet, from all that I have heard concerning the boy, he could be no threat to you or to any man in Turān. It is said that, though as handsome as a prince, he is no better than half-witted, simpler by far in his mind than even the peasants among whom he dwells. How could such a one be a threat to the great lord of Turān or to his empire? It would be a cruel and an unnecessary deed, and unpleasing to divine Ormuzd, to put to death a harmless idiot boy.'

Afrāsib's heart lightened a little at these words of his general. He smiled. 'It would indeed be cruel,' he agreed. 'Cruel and deserving of the anger of Ormuzd.' Yet then, when he had thought a little further, he went on, 'Though what you have been told concerning the boy is doubtless true—for why should any man trouble himself to lie about the wits of a shepherd lad?—it would be for us to act with no more sense than the boy himself is said to show, to accept a rumour as the truth without seeing for ourselves how things stand, would it not?'

'It would indeed, lord Emperor,' agreed Pirān, hiding his concern.

'Fetch the boy to me secretly, good Pirān, that I may see him and question him, and make judgement on his wits for myself.'

Pirān bowed low. 'It shall be done.'

Greatly troubled in his mind as to the outcome of Afrāsib's demand, Pirān left the imperial palace and rode unwillingly towards the mountains in search of Khosroes. He found him at work among the sheep with several of the other shepherds. As Pirān called him aside, Khosroes saw at once from his grave looks that some ill had befallen. 'All is not well with you,' he said.

'Indeed, all is not well,' replied Pirān. 'The Emperor has demanded that you be taken to him.'

'My kindest and best of friends,' said the young prince, 'it had to come one day, that hour when I and my grandfather stand face to face.'

'It could mean death for you,' said Pirān heavily. 'Yet be guided by me and there is a chance that, by the grace of Ormuzd, you may escape so cruel a fate.'

'What would you have me do?' asked Khosroes.

'I have lied to the Emperor and told him that you are lacking in your wits. If you can indeed convince him of this, then you may well be safe from him.'

'Do not fear,' Khosroes assured him. 'I shall not betray us. He shall find me as foolish as a stone, and think me as much danger to him as a new-born babe.'

Pirān gave Khosroes garments more fitting to one of royal birth than the rough sheepskins he wore, and mounted him upon a fine horse; then, with a princely escort they rode to the imperial palace. Somehow, in the manner of such rumours, word had reached the people of the city that the commander of the army was bringing to the Emperor a boy who was a long-lost son of Siyāvush; and they crowded in the streets to cheer him as he passed, for Siyāvush had been as much loved by the people of Turān as he had been dear to the Persians. Young Khosroes was moved by such a show of affection; but Pirān was disturbed lest it should come to the ears of Afrāsib and anger him.

As they were dismounting to be received and welcomed by the palace guards, Pirān whispered rapidly to the boy, 'Remember, give him a foolish answer to all his questions. If, say, he speaks of battles, give him an answer concerning wedding feasts. Speak only nonsense to him: your life depends on it.'

There was no time for further words, so Khosroes, with fast beating heart, only nodded to him in reply, and smiled as reassuringly as he could, while they were being led to the throne-room.

Afrāsib looked searchingly at the boy who stood before him. 'In looks he is indeed a perfect prince, and one most fitted by his appearance to wear a crown,' he said at last. And although to the courtiers and the guards who heard him, it seemed as though his words were a high compliment, Pirān alone knew them for the threat they were.

Afrāsib smiled at Khosroes and spoke gently to him. 'Do not fear, young shepherd, though you find yourself in the palace of the Emperor. You are welcome here. Now, tell me, how many sheep are there in the flock in your charge?'

Khosroes stared at him in silence for a few moments, as though he did not perfectly understand the question; then he gave a sudden smile —as foolish a smile as he could feign—and said, 'I would hunt the wild beasts, but that there are none. And, besides, I have neither bow nor arrows.'

Afrāsib seemed to Khosroes to be pleased by this answer. He asked further, 'How has your life been, boy? Has your fate been good or ill?'

'Where roams the leopard, master, there men's hearts are clawed.' Khosroes spoke earnestly, as though he repeated to the Emperor a proverb of great wisdom.

'Tell me,' said Afrāsib, 'what means the name of Persia to you?' When Khosroes only stared at him as though uncomprehendingly, he went on, 'Who are your parents, shepherd? Come, tell me the names of your father and mother.'

After a silence during which it seemed that Khosroes pondered carefully, he shook his head and replied to the question. 'A barking dog cannot bring down a lion, master. Did you not know?'

'If the chance were offered you, would you go to live in Persia? To dwell in the palace of the Great King Kāvus himself and pass your days like a prince?' Afrāsib leant forward awaiting Khosroes' answer as though much depended on it—as, indeed, it did. 'Come, shepherd, tell me truly.'

Khosroes said eagerly, 'Master, do you know what I saw the night before last night? Shall I tell you? I saw a horseman riding fast over the plain in the moonlight. Was that not a fine sight to see?'

Afrāsib smiled, pleased greatly and soothed by Khosroes' replies to his questions. He glanced towards Pirān, nodding his head a little, as though confirming that Piran had indeed been told the truth about the wits of this son of Siyāvush. Then he turned again to Khosroes. 'Here is another question for you, shepherd. Tell me, would you care to learn to read and write?' Khosroes once more stared at him as though he did not understand; and after a minute or so, Afrāsib said, 'Well, it is no matter. If you do not know what reading and writing are, how can you tell whether you would wish to read and write or not? But now, this is my very last question, boy, think carefully and answer it truthfully. Would you not wish to be revenged upon your enemies?' While he spoke, and while he awaited his reply, Afrāsib watched Khosroes very closely.

After what seemed a very long silence both to Afrāsib and to Pirān, Khosroes said, 'There was no cream on the milk this morning. Was that not strange?'

Afrāsib laughed aloud. A heavy weight had been lifted from his heart. He turned to Pirān. 'Rumour did not lie, my friend. He is indeed entirely without wits. I ask him concerning his head and he replies concerning his feet. He will never make his mark in life either for good or for ill. It is not among men of his stamp that avengers are to be found. Poor child, let him leave his shepherding and go to dwell with his mother. It will bring joy to her; and to him, also, I trust. See that he is well attended, good Pirān, as befits the son of a princess of Turān. Let him lack for nothing: gold, horses, slaves, as well as all that a boy's heart may desire.'

Thus Afrāsib eased his conscience concerning his grandson; and if his heart was lighter than it had been for many a day as he watched Pirān take Khosroes by the hand to lead him from the throne-room, so also were the hearts of Pirān and Khosroes lighter by the weight of the dread of death that departed from them even as they left Afrāsib's presence.

So, to her great comfort, Khosroes went to live in the palace where Farangis had dwelt in seclusion since the day he had been taken from her and sent among the shepherds; and for a short time all seemed well with them, and they had no fears for Khosroes' life.

But young Khosroes was not to remain unthreatened for long. The Great King Kāvus, in vengeance for the murder of Siyāvush, sent an army of chosen warriors against Turān; and Rustem, eager to avenge his one-time pupil, went with them. When Afrāsib learnt that the dreaded champion Rustem was come against him when he was all unprepared for an attack, he made ready with speed to leave the imperial palace with his courtiers, his treasure and his wives, for a place of greater safety, farther from the Persian border. To Pirān, his commander-in-chief, he left it to call an army together and prepare a defence, and fight his battles for him. 'And,' he said to Pirān, 'it were best that young Khosroes be slain immediately, before the Persians can reach him and carry him with them on their campaign as a reminder to them of the death of Siyāvush, and an inspiration to all who oppose me. Khosroes must die, and that as soon as may be. See to it for me, good Pirān.'

But Pirān protested against the command; and so earnestly he pleaded for Khosroes' life, and so much in fear for his own life was Afrāsib, that, between Pirān's pleas and Afrāsib's haste to be gone to a safer place, Khosroes' life was spared and he was instead, at Pirān's suggestion, sent with his mother to Khotān, Pirān's own kingdom to the east of the empire of Turān, many hundred leagues from the Persian border.

Afrāsib's fears were realized. The Turanian army, led by Pirān, was unable to hold back the Persian advance, but was forced to retreat before it, leaving a wide tract of land, north and east of the border between the two empires, in the hands of the Persians, who triumphantly took possession of Afrāsib's palace in his capital. There, on the orders of Kāvus, Rustem remained as regent, to rule, in the name of the Great King, and King of Kings, those parts of Turān which had fallen to the Persian army.

For seven years Rustem dwelt in Turān, while Afrāsib fretted and tormented himself with impotent anger, just beyond the reach of the Persians, who were content with the land they had gained and who, save for a few forays northward and eastward, let him be. During this time, far away in Khotān, Khosroes grew to a fine young man; and as he grew, so also grew his longing, fostered by his mother Farangis, to see his father avenged.

Then, after seven years, Kāvus, who was growing old, bade Rustem return to Persia. 'I am no longer young,' he said to him, 'and I must consider a successor. Who better to rule over the empire of Persia when I am dead and gone, than the son of my Siyāvush?' Rustem agreed with him, as did most of his counsellors and lords, and so Kāvus sent the warrior Giv, the bold son of Gudarz and one of his most trusted generals, with a few brave men, into Turān, to go all about the empire, in the guise of peaceful travellers, to search for Khosroes, that they might bring him to his grandfather.

After many months of searching they found him in far-away Khotān. Giv made himself known to the young prince and told him of the wishes of Kāvus, and secretly and swiftly Khosroes and his mother fled from Khotān with Giv. Their journey to Persia was difficult and dangerous, for, once Afrāsib learnt from his spies in Khotān that Khosroes had disappeared and was gone no one knew whither, he sent men in pursuit, to pick up his trail and slay him the moment he was found. Piran—whom Afrāsib blamed not only for Khosroes' escape, but also for the fact that Khosroes had lived to become a danger—was deprived of his command of the imperial army and banished from all other regions of the Turanian empire, save his own land of Khotān.

In spite of Afrāsib and those who hunted them relentlessly, Giv and Khosroes and his mother reached Persia safely, where, much pleased by the noble appearance and regal manner of his grandson,

Kāvus proclaimed him his heir and successor. Rustem, Giv, Gudarz, and all his other counsellors and generals, save only Tus, agreed and gladly accepted Khosroes as the future Great King, and King of Kings. Tus alone protested, insisting that a son of Kāvus named Feriburz—with whom Tus was on the best of terms, and from whom he hoped for favours, once Feriburz was crowned—had the greater claim. But, Tus being his only supporter, the rights of Feriburz were set aside.

Then Kāvus, being old and weary, handed over to Khosroes his sceptre and the golden tiara and bade him seat himself upon the golden imperial throne, take over the rule of the empire and avenge upon the Emperor Afrāsib the wrongs which all Persia had suffered at his hands. Amid rejoicing, Khosroes did as he was bidden by his grandfather, assuming imperial rights and splendour; and, moreover, he swore by divine Ormuzd and by the sacred fire, that never would he touch the hand of Afrāsib in friendship, but would avenge—though it took him all his life—the murder of Siyāvush and Afrāsib's many other ill deeds.

15: Forud of Kalāt

STRAIGHTWAY after his accession the Great King Khosroes called together the whole army of Persia, and soon the plain before the capital was loud with the clamour of men at arms and horses, and bright with banners, coloured pavilions and glinting, polished armour of bronze and iron. When all were gathered, the royal elephant, with a high throne upon its back, was fetched and made to kneel; and Khosroes ascended and seated himself upon the throne. On his head was the tall, glittering tiara, the crown of the Great Kings of Persia; and about his neck, below the stiff, curled regal beard, he wore a jewelled collar; on his arms were bracelets set with gems and from his ears hung jewels, while about his waist there glinted a gem-set silver belt. In the sunlight, seated high upon the royal elephant, so young and so handsome, with all his jewels flashing splendidly, he looked to his people like a good spirit sent to earth by Ormuzd, rather than a man.

At a sign from him, the brazen battle-trumpets blared forth and the drums sounded; huge frame-drums and smaller kettle-drums, all rolling like thunder. Every man fell silent and stood to listen. At another sign from Khosroes all the warriors of the great empire of Persia, in their own troops and led by their own subject-king or prince, passed in review before the Great King, the banners of each separate province or kingdom flying above their heads. Loud as was the sound of the trumpets and the drums, even louder was the cheering of all men for their new young overlord.

When every man had passed in review, Khosroes made a sign that all should be silent, then he called to him Tus, the general. Before those assembled there, he handed Tus a royal seal, proclaiming him the commander-in-chief and leader of the imperial army of Persia, and bade all men obey his orders as though he had been the Great King himself. For though it was not unknown to Khosroes that Tus had opposed his crowning as successor to Kāvus, Tus was a noted, older, warrior and reputed to be a most able leader, also; and Khosroes knew well the value of such a man in time of war.

The warriors all shouted and cheered for Tus as their new commander; and again the drums rolled and the trumpets sounded. Then, addressing Tus, Khosroes said, 'Be loyal to me and act ever as I would act. On your march, see that no harm comes to the

innocent folk through whose lands you pass. Let no man steal from the farmers and the peasants, and spare any town or village where no man takes arms against you. Let it never be said that the army of Persia is a horde of savage wolves and ruthless tigers, rather than an army of brave and honourable warriors.'

Tus bowed low before Khosroes. 'I shall obey you in all things, Great King. It shall indeed be as though you yourself led your army against Afrāsib.'

Khosroes smiled, pleased by this reply. 'There is one more demand which I would make of you, good Tus.'

'Speak, Great King, and King of Kings, and it shall be done', said Tus, and awaited Khosroes' words.

Now, it had happened that Siyāvush had taken as one of his wives Jarira, a daughter of Pirān, commander of the Turanian army, who had been so good a friend to Khosroes' mother. Jarira was herself the mother of a son, Forud, born, like Khosroes, after his father's death. This young man ruled over the small Turanian province of Kalāt, not far from the Persian border, paying tribute to the Emperor Afrāsib, yet, for the sake of his father, wishing only peace with Persia and having little love for Afrāsib.

This half-brother of his now came to Khosroes' mind, and he said to Tus, 'I have been told that, on your march against Afrāsib, you will come to a place where there is a choice of roads. One, the shorter, leads across the desert. The other, which is longer, goes by the mountain pass that runs through the kingdom of Kalāt. In Kalāt rules my brother Forud. I would not have him committed to this war on either side, to suffer and, perhaps, to die. I charge you, good Tus, take the road across the desert and let Forud continue to dwell in peace, and may Ormuzd grant him a long and happy life.'

Again Tus bowed his head. 'It shall be so, Great King. I will take the desert road, as you command. War shall not reach to Kalāt through any deed of mine.' And Khosroes was satisfied by his words.

Preceded by the huge drum-elephants and with the fluttering Banner of Kāva held above him, Tus, magnificent in shining brazen armour, led the imperial army of Persia over the borderlands on to Turanian soil. They went unopposed and swiftly, by ways which were easy and allowed of speed, until they reached that place of which Khosroes had spoken, at which a choice of roads lay before them. One way led across a desert, dry and stony; the other, greener, path lay through the mountain pass of Kalāt, where the land was cultivated and fertile, and there were streams of clear water and trees to give shade to men and beasts. The drum-elephants in the van of the army were halted at this spot, to wait until Tus and those who escorted the Banner of Kāva came up with them. 'Which path are we to take, lord commander?' Tus was asked.

Tus looked first along one way and then along the other, and he said to Gudarz the general, father of Giv, who rode beside him, 'The track across the desert is short, yet very hard; I know it of old. Likewise, I know the mountain pass which runs through Kalāt. It is the longer road and it climbs uphill and down again every half league, yet there is abundant water and fresh herbage for horse and elephant; and on the mountain road we can rest where and when we will. If we take the shorter road, we must take it in a single march, for we cannot halt to rest until we have left the waterless and barren desert lands safely behind us.' Tus raised his voice and called to those who followed him, 'Pass the word back: we take the mountain road through Kalāt.'

'The Great King bade you take the desert road and avoid his brother's kingdom,' he was reminded by Gudarz, who had been standing near when Khosroes had spoken of Forud.

'The Great King is far off in his palace and cannot see by which path we march. He need not vex himself over the matter,' Tus said shortly, adding, 'And neither need you vex yourself over it, friend Gudarz.' He gave a brief, sharp laugh; and Gudarz shrugged his shoulders and protested no more.

The drum-elephants moved off; and after them, Tus and the Banner of Kāva; and after him, all the Persian army, marching on towards the little mountain kingdom of Kalāt.

From a high outpost, King Forud's guards who watched the road which led through Kalāt, saw the approach of an army: elephants, horses, men, chariots, and baggage wagons, a long column, crawling like a snake along the narrow mountain road. A man ran swiftly with word of it to his king.

Young Forud in his palace—built half-way up the mountainside, and more a fortress than a palace—was in the company of his mother Jarira, the daughter of Pirān. At the words of the messenger, he frowned, troubled. 'A great army, you say, and coming from the direction of Persia. What can this mean?'

Jarira laid a hand upon his arm. 'Go swiftly to an outpost from where you can see the road for yourself and make out the emblems on the banners of those who approach, my son. Take with you good old Tokhār, for he knows well the emblems of the noble families of Turān and Persia alike—and besides, his counsel is ever good.'

Hastily Forud made ready and rode for the high peak beside the narrow pass which was the gateway into Kalāt. With him, as his mother had advised, rode Tokhār, his chief counsellor. After a time, as it drew ever closer, Forud and Tokhār, shading their eyes against the sun, were able to make out the emblems of some of the many banners carried by the approaching army.

'That is indeed the imperial army of Persia, as I feared it would prove to be,' said Tokhār. 'See, that is the Banner of Kāva which is carried before it.'

'The imperial army of Persia, and it stretches along the road farther than an eagle could see,' said Forud heavily. 'The whole army of all Persia, and marching against the Emperor Afrāsib, without a doubt. But what care I for the quarrels of Afrāsib my overlord, and Khosroes my father's son? I have no love for Afrāsib; and Khosroes is unknown to me. Yet I am a king, Tokhār, though my kingdom be small. Shall the enemies of Turān pass through my land unchecked?' And he placed his men across the narrow road in token of protest.

A certain distance from the outpost where Forud and Tokhār waited, Tus halted the army and sent a noted warrior, Bahrām—a kinsman of Giv and Gudarz—to parley with the men who stood at the pass and inquire who they might be. Forud and Tokhār watched Bahrām as he came.

'The man comes openly and without fear,' said Forud. 'Who is he, Tokhār, this bold Persian?'

'I do not recognize his banner,' the older man replied. 'Yet I would say it was one of the banners of the family of Gudarz.'

When Bahrām was close enough for his voice to be heard by those who so warily watched him come, he called out, 'Who are you, you few who dare to stand there in the path of so mighty an army?'

Forud called back, 'Do you threaten me, stranger? Seek to pick no quarrels with me, for I am no wild ass, all braying words and little courage. Nor can you, I think, for all your bragging, be considered a lion in valour. So let us keep the peace between us, like wise men. And since you are the invaders, marching through my land without cause, it is for you to name yourselves. Tell me, who are the leaders of your army, and what king sends them to Kalāt?'

Bahrām did not give him an answer immediately; but after they had cautiously questioned each other further, he said in a less hostile manner, 'Our great army is the imperial army of Persia, under the command of Tus, appointed by Khosroes, the Great King, and King of Kings, and sent forth by him against the Emperor Afrāsib. For the Great King has much for which he seeks vengeance upon Afrāsib: the despoiling of the borderlands, dead men and widowed wives and orphans, and the cruel murder of his father Siyāvush.'

'Siyāvush was my father, also,' said Forud. 'I, too, have dreamt of the day when I should avenge him. Go, tell your commander Tus that he is welcome in Kalāt. Let him and his brother-generals come in peace to my palace and receive what entertainment I can offer them. And then, when the feasting is done, I and my small army shall ride with the men of Persia against our common enemy.'

Bahrām said slowly, 'Tus did not send me to make alliance with you, but only to ask your name and why you sought to prevent his passage over the mountains. Yet I will tell him your words and hope that he will receive them well. But Tus is a curious man, of many moods; often obstinate and seldom owning any to be his master. He it was who supported the claims of Feriburz, the son of Great King Kāvus, against the claims of your brother Khosroes. I believe that in his heart Tus would still see Feriburz in Khosroes' place. So be warned by me: do not too easily trust in the words of Tus, whatever answer he may send you. If I bring his reply, you may believe in it. But if another carries back his message, then beware of treachery. Meanwhile, until I or another come to you, spend the minutes wisely, strengthening your guard on the road and barring strongly the gates of your town and fortress.'

'You have my thanks for your counsel, good Bahrām,' said Forud, and with courteous ceremony they parted. Then Forud drew up all his guards in the narrow pass; and he sent a man running to the town, both to bid the rest of his warriors come to him at once, and to warn the townsfolk to fasten the gates against all comers.

When Bahrām returned to Tus and told him of Forud's message of friendship and his offer to join with the Persians in their fight against Afrāsib, Tus flew into a rage. 'A single warrior, with a handful of men at his back, and you have allowed yourself to be worsted by him. Like a coward you refrained from combat and instead parleyed like a fool. And now you bring me his impudent words instead of his head. This wretch may claim to be a son of Siyāvush—we have only his word for that—yet his mother was a Turanian, and we desire and need no Turanian allies in this war.' He turned and called to those who stood near by, 'Is there any among you who is a true man and no weakling, who will climb the mountain and slay this insolent Forud for me?'

Two young warriors, one of them the son of Tus and the other his daughter's husband, immediately stood forth. 'Give us your leave to do this deed for you, lord father,' they said eagerly.

Tus was pleased and glanced with scorn at Bahrām while he praised the two young men for their spirit. But Bahrām went to them and spoke earnestly, seeking to persuade them from their intention; but they would not hear him. Well armed and swaggering aggressively they set off, mouthing threats against Forud. He saw them coming with their weapons ready and he heard their threats; and at the sight and the sound he had no need to remember Bahrām's warning to him: these men plainly bore him no peaceful message from Tus. Since he who strikes the first blow often has the advantage even though he be outnumbered, he wasted no time, but with two well-aimed arrows he slew them both as they came.

Seeing his two sons thus shot and slain, Tus was beside himself with regret and rage. He called for his weapons and armour; and when he was prepared for combat, mounted on his stout war-horse, he set off towards the pass.

'That is Tus himself, commander of all the Persian army, who comes like a storm-cloud against you. Have a care, my king,' said Tokhār.

'Let him come,' said Forud. 'And let it be for him to have a care, for he comes to his death.'

'Behind him, my king, march thirty thousand Persian warriors.'

'What of it?' Forud replied. 'The few brave warriors of Kalāt are all I need to hold the pass against an army of twice that size.'

This might well have been so, and Forud and his small band of loyal men might indeed have held off Tus and the Persian army until such time as Tus decided that the cost of taking the mountain road was higher than he cared to pay, ordered a retreat and marched instead across the desert. But it was old Tokhār who counselled otherwise, and since Forud had ever respected his advice, it was Tokhār's counsel which in the end was to prevail.

'If you rashly seek to oppose Tus here, in the pass,' Tokhār said, 'there will be thirty thousand warriors who will bring the very mountains tumbling down and stamp them into a pathway broad enough for their march. They will move onward over our bodies without pausing and take Kalāt. Not a stone of your palace will be left; not a single man remain to remember the name of Forud, his king. Let us leave the pass to the enemy and retire to Kalāt and make secure our defences. Thus alone have we any hope of success.'

'If I were to slay Tus as he comes against me, the whole Persian army, lacking its commander, might well be thrown into confusion,' said Forud, taking up his bow.

But he was moved when Tokhār said, 'Tus is the Great King Khosroes' chosen commander. Khosroes is your brother; would you so lightly slay the man whom he has chosen to honour? The man who is to avenge for him your father's murder?'

After a long moment of silence, Forud said, 'Good Tokhār, you do well to remind me of my brother Khosroes and my duty to the memory of my father. I would not be undutiful, and I would not give a brother cause for grief, stranger though he be to me. Let us do as you advise and return without delay to the town. Within the fortress we can well withstand a siege until such time as the Persians tire of inaction and turn back to march against Afrāsib by another road.'

So it was that, out of charity towards his unknown brother Khosroes, Forud took his counsellor's advice, and thereby lost his own life.

Forud and the men of Kalāt closed themselves up in their strong fortress and the Persian army encamped uneasily on the steep mountainside about the town. Each day one brave warrior, a champion among the Persians, came alone to meet Forud in single combat; and each one of them Forud slew. Then Bizhān, the son of the noble courtier and general Giv, and a grandson of Gudarz, swore that on the morrow he would lead his own small band of chosen warriors against Forud and the champions of Kalāt. And he swore, moreover, that he would not fail as all the other Persian warriors had failed. He sent his challenge to Forud, who eagerly accepted it.

That night Jarira, Forud's mother, had an evil dream. Believing it to be an omen of ill fortune, she went at dawning to Forud and said, 'Alas, my son, I fear for you. Last night I dreamt of naught but disaster to your people and death to you.'

'Good mother,' Forud replied, 'do not weep for me. My father perished young; if it is fated that I should have a like destiny to his, then your tears are of no avail. If this son of Giv should slay me, why then, he slays me and I shall have died like a brave man, as befits your son and a son of Siyāvush, and as befits a grandson of good old Pirān. I have no desire for death; yet even less do I desire mercy from those who have proclaimed themselves our enemies.' He armed himself, in spite of his mother's pleas; and with the best and boldest of his men, went forth to oppose Bizhān.

They met, two bands of brave men with their young leaders, on the steep mountainside where fighting was not easy, and horses many a time lost their footing on the loose pebbles and flung their riders on to the sharp rocks. The gallant champions of Kalāt, spurred on by the example of their young king, fought like mountain lions in defence of their homeland; but they were outmatched by the followers of Bizhān.

After a time, Forud stood with only a hand's counting of men about him, all his other warriors having been slain. Seeing this, Bizhān, who still had a score of men, said to his uncle Rāhām, who fought beside him, 'Soon there will be none left to oppose us save this princeling, Forud, who battles like a true hero. When only he is left standing, surely even he must retreat before us. Let us send men to hide behind the rocks at his back, between him and the gates of the town. That way he may be taken by surprise and slain.'

This was done, and it soon happened as Bizhān had expected: Forud alone of all the finest warriors of Kalāt still lived. He made one last onslaught against Bizhān, striking him a great blow with his battle-axe upon the leathern helmet, strengthened with iron plates and decorated with silver, which he wore, so that Bizhān fell senseless. Then swiftly Forud urged his horse back, up the slope towards the safety of his fortress. But he was prepared for no attack in his retreat, save from his rear, and thus, as Bizhān had hoped, he was taken by surprise by the men who lay in ambush. Surrounded, he fought valiantly but vainly. Rāhām came upon him from behind, and with his sharp sword thrust at his shoulder and right side, so that his right arm drooped uselessly and he could no longer hold a weapon. Then someone struck down his horse from under him. He fell heavily upon the rocky ground, but, somehow, escaped from the Persian warriors who pressed all about him in attack, and made his way, as swiftly as he might for the pain of his wounds, towards the fortress. A number of townsfolk ran out to him, half-led and half-carried him to safety and barred the gates once more against the rejoicing enemy. Forud sank down in a swoon and his mother and her women, with tears and wailing, came to him to tend him. But they saw that he was hurt to death, and that not all their care could avail to save his life. So that he might die like a king in his royal splendour, they carried him gently to his carven throne, and taking off his helmet, set his crown upon his head and his gilded regal-beard at his chin.

Slowly and wearily Forud opened his eyes to the sight of his mother's tears, and saw and heard how her women tore their hair and mourned for him as though he were already dead. In little more than a whisper he spoke to them. 'Soon Tus will enter Kalāt, there being no warriors left to protect the town. All men he will put to the sword, my treasure he will take for himself, and all the women he will divide amongst his warriors. My dearest mother, let me die knowing that you will never be any man's slave. Let Tus find no living women when he enters my palace.' With the effort of speech his cheeks grew paler, his voice faltered, his crowned head dropped on his breast and he slipped from his throne; and so he died.

Jarira, a true daughter of a great general, and a true mother of a brave warrior, gave orders that all was to be as her son had wished; moreover, she commanded that all the horses in Kalāt were to be hamstrung or slain, that they might never bear an enemy of Kalāt into battle. Then, when she had seen all done as she had bidden, she knelt beside Forud's body with a dagger in her hand. 'I would have died with you even had you not asked it, my dearest child. I have no wish to outlive you by one hour.' She stabbed herself through the heart, and her body fell across his and lay still.

The defences having been broken by Bizhān and his men, Tus with his generals, and with all those of his champions whom Forud had not slain, entered Kalāt. Tus was loudly triumphant; but Bahrām, and many others with him, mourned the death of so brave a young king, and regretted that he had not lived to ride with them against Afrāsib.

'He should have been our ally,' they said. 'This useless slaughter need not have been. It will make sad tidings for the Great King Khosroes.'

16: The Defeat of Persia

As Forud had known he would, Tus sacked Kalāt, slaying the men and seizing everything of value. He then led the army along the mountain road towards the plain beyond, ravaging all hill farms and villages that lay in his path, against the orders of Khosroes. He saw no need for haste; the mountain slopes were fertile and there was abundance of fodder for the horses and the elephants, and game in plenty and farm crops and cattle for the troops. But, not being weatherwise, he lingered too long upon the mountainside, so that the first, unexpectedly early snowfall of autumn took him by surprise. The fall was heavy. Snow covered the baggage wagons and chariots and the pavilions overnight; it changed the green and pleasant aspect of the foot-hills to a terrifying wasteland. For drink the army had only the snow that could hardly melt in ice-cold mouths, and for food there was nothing save the starving horses which Tus rashly ordered his men to slaughter. For seven days this weather lasted, fearful weather such as no man among the Persians had before endured while under arms. And then on the eighth day the leaden sky was suddenly split open by the rays of the sun, which they had not glimpsed for all the past week. In the space of an hour the sky had cleared and the sun was blazing down on them as though from the bottom of an inverted brazen bowl. The snow melted into rushing streams that poured down the mountainside, and everything—wagons, chariots, pavilions, arms, drowned men and beasts—was swept along upon the flood. Too late, Tus brought his starving and bedraggled army down to the plain. Days later, when the imperial army of Persia had in part recovered from the cruelty of the weather, Tus gave word for their march onward through Afrāsib's land.

Despoiling and plundering as they went, they replaced, by looting, the horses they had slaughtered; and as they met with little resistance from the Turanian countryfolk, and as they easily overcame the few local Turanian warriors who came almost alone against them, the spirits of the Persians soon rose and, forgetting the terrors of the snow and hunger, they became daily more hopeful of an easy victory. As for Tus, he already saw Afrāsib kneeling in the dust before him, his crown fallen from his head; and puffed up with pride at the small successes he had so far achieved, he became over-confident, slowing down his progress and thereby leaving time for the Turanian army to make ready; encamping too long in one place; and allowing a rash degree of slackness among his warriors. Evening after evening, following their commander's example, his men stuffed themselves with stolen food and caroused on looted wine; and after, slept heavily until long past dawn in a camp where even the very sentries snored at their posts unchecked.

Alone of all the great army, the generals Giv and his father Gudarz remained sober and vigilant, for ever trying without effect to warn Tus against his folly and vainly attempting to argue with their fellow-generals. Giv's warnings failed to move even his brave son Bizhān, who had led the victorious assault against Kalāt. Bizhān only smiled and said, 'You fret yourself without need, my father. We are conquering Turān and conquering easily. We have cause for feasting and mirth. Now it is the time for wine, not war.'

Day after day word came to Afrāsib of the almost unopposed advance of the Persian army. Rashly slow though its progress might be for its own safety, it was too fast for Afrāsib's peace of mind. Angrily he sent to Khotān, ordering Pirān back from banishment and restoring to him the command of the army. Barely allowing time for messages to be sent summoning the subject-kings from the provinces, Afrāsib demanded of Pirān, 'How much longer will you permit our enemies to despoil our land? Days since, I bade you raise our standards and call together the warriors of Turān. Why this delay, this faint-heartedness, this cowardice of yours? You are no longer young, I know; but I did not believe you in your dotage yet. Perhaps I was mistaken, and should have given command of my army to a younger, abler man.'

Pirān, bold warrior though he still was, was indeed growing old; and with age there had come to him the realization that peace brings more benefits and happiness to men than war. Yet at Afrāsib's threats he made speed to gather troops for the defence of Turān, though, at the same time, deploring that once again those age-old enemies, Persia and Turān, would be at open war. At first his heart was not in the task of preparing a defence, though he loyally obeyed his Emperor; and then word came to him of the deaths of his daughter Jarira and his grandson Forud, and the sacking of Kalāt; and immediately, grief and anger firing him, his only desire became the destruction of those who had been the destroyers of his own flesh and blood.

With the greatest speed he led the army, its numbers equalling

the numbers of the army of Persia, by secret, hidden ways towards that place where Tus then lay encamped. A few leagues from the spot, he sent scouts by night to spy upon the Persians. The scouts returned with stories almost unbelievable, of a silent, sleeping camp, unguarded and at ease.

The next day Pirān ordered a march to within a short distance of

the Persian camp, and there he waited and rested his men until nightfall. Then, by darkness, the Turanians attacked. In all the Persian camp, Giv alone lay unsleeping and wary, and so was the first to know of the assault. He leapt up, mounted the saddled and bridled horse which he ever kept ready beside his pavilion, and rode from end to end of the camp, calling out that they were attacked, and endeavouring to raise an effective defence. But the Persians, taken utterly by surprise, could put up little opposition. All night Pirān and the Turanians slaughtered men and burnt down pavilions and baggage wagons, retiring victorious and elated just before the approach of dawn.

The risen sun shone down upon a scene of desolation and of horror, in the midst of which stood Giv and his father Gudarz, surveying the Persian dead and wounded through eyes dimmed by tears. Tus, shocked and shaken by the knowledge that his was the blame for that night's events, had lost his reason and could only sit upon the ground, rocking himself from side to side and muttering foolishnesses, staring with blank eyes at any who addressed him.

Giv sent a man, known to him as a swift runner, with word of the disaster to the Great King Khosroes; and then he and Gudarz and Bizhān gathered together the remnants of the army and retreated towards the mountains. Despondently they drew up their lines upon the foot-hills, while Pirān and his men did not even bestir themselves to follow after them, despising the feeble resistance of which alone the Persians would have been capable.

When Khosroes learnt of the defeat, and who was answerable for it, he sent messengers at once to Tus, demanding his return. When Tus, his wits still wandering, stood before him, Khosroes, white with wrath, spoke furiously. 'Are you not ashamed to look into the face of any man or woman of Persia, unworthy wretch? I gave you command of my army—could I have honoured any man more highly than that?—yet you defied me and flouted my orders. You led the army through Kalāt and you slew my brother Forud, though I had forbidden it. With singing and wine-bibbing you celebrated your petty victories, and it is therefore no petty victory which Afrāsib celebrates today. Upon your miserable head is the blood of scores of Persian warriors. You do not deserve to live another hour. Yet, because you are descended from Minucher—that bravest of all warrior-kings—and because in the past you have served your country well, and because you now stand before me witless and crazed, I will spare your worthless life. Go! For your remaining days your own house shall be your prison, and your conscience your most cruel gaoler.'

Then, as commander-in-chief of the army, in place of Tus, Khosroes appointed Feriburz, that son of Kāvus whose claims to the kingship of Persia, Tus had supported. Feriburz set off at once to the mountain camp where Giv and Gudarz had taken charge while they waited for word from Khosroes. When Feriburz saw the piteous plight of the Persian army, he said, 'Unless we have time in which to recover ourselves before we return to the field of battle—to call together fresh men, to replace weapons lost and broken, and to heal our wounded—then we are already as good as dead.' And he sent Rāhām, the son of Gudarz, to Pirān with a letter requesting a truce which should last a full month.

At the Turanian camp Rāhām was led at once to the pavilion of Pirān. Standing before Pirān, suddenly Rāhām was afraid lest the Turanian commander would not respect his state as herald, and might have him slain without even listening to the message which he brought. But he had no need of fear, for old Pirān was not only a warrior of note, he was a man of honour. He greeted Rāhām as he might have greeted a friend, with compliments and courtesy, asking him how he did and bidding him be seated; and Rāhām knew then, without a doubt, that his life was in no danger from this noble old man. Alone with Pirān, he gave him the message of Feriburz.

After a few moments of thought, Pirān said, 'It was your Great King who forced this fight on us, your army which invaded our land. Like a savage wolf has Tus, your commander, ravaged the countryside, sparing none. Well did he deserve his just defeat at our hands. And now the Persians beg for a month of peace, that they may recover themselves before they come out to battle again.' He paused a moment, but Rāhām had no words with which to answer his accusations, for he spoke only the truth. Then Pirān went on, 'Yet, in spite of this, and since Tus, who was so much to blame, no longer leads your army, and since it is Feriburz, the son of Kāvus, who asks it of me, I will grant the truce you seek. Go, tell Feriburz that no one of my warriors will take arms against the men of Persia for the space of one month from this day. When that time is past, I and the brave men of Turān shall be ready to meet him in battle, if it is a continuance of this war that he desires. But tell him also, noble Rāhām, that if at that time the Persians prefer peace, then let him send to me to say so, and he may withdraw with all his men to Persia, safely and in no fear that we shall harass his retreat.'

Gratefully Rāhām heard the old man and thanked him in the name of Feriburz and all the Persian army. Then Pirān gave a fine and costly robe to Rāhām, as though the younger man had been a guest who had come to him in time of peace, and he wished him all fortune as he bade him farewell with gentle courtesy.

True to his word, Pirān, with all the Turanian army, waited idly in camp for the promised month; while Feriburz spent the days in hastily calling together men to take the place of those who had been slain, in gathering supplies and fodder, and in replacing the horses which had been lost. He poured out gold in buying all that was needed, and he sought fresh troops everywhere; and both to such good effect that when the month was past, the Persian army was once again as strong as it had been on that unlucky day when Khosroes had given it into the charge of Tus.

On the very morning the truce was ended, Feriburz gave the order to move against the Turanians, and the army set off. Pirān's spies brought him word that the enemy was on the march, and he sent his orders around the Turanian camp. Soon his men were on their way to meet their foes.

Eagerly and fiercely the two great armies met on a wide plain. The clash of weapons, the neighing of war-horses, the wild trumpeting of battle-elephants, and the shouts and cries of men resounded everywhere. Swords flashed in the sunlight, spears dripped redly, while arrows flew like flocks of countless, flesh-hungry birds.

The men on both sides fought bravely; but whereas the Persians sought only conquest, the Turanians strove in defence of their own violated land, and this gave a greater resolution to their efforts and greater strength to their hands. Before the day was out the Persians were yielding, pressed back towards the foot-hills. Feriburz gave the order for retreat, and with the larger part of the army that remained to him, he rode fast for their mountain camp.

Only Giv and Gudarz and Bizhān and a bare few score men, brave warriors all, stood firm, and watched in dismay their commander's retreat. As he saw the bright Banner of Kāva disappear as swiftly as the tired horses could gallop, old Gudarz said bitterly, 'If Feriburz our commander retreats, then who are we to do otherwise?' and he turned his horse's head for the hills.

But Giv said to him, 'Dear father, my comrade of many battles, would you shame our noble name? What if it is our fate to die today? Let us at least die facing our enemies as befits two warriors of Persia. And why should we die? Might we not fight and live instead? Is there not an old saying, that if two loving comrades-in-arms fight back to back, a mountain will be to them no more than a little heap of sand? If Pirān and the Turanians are a mountain set upon overwhelming us today, let us raze that mountain to the level of this plain, and scatter it as a handful of sand.'

The two of them then rallied those who had remained with them, and standing close together in a little group, they awaited the next Turanian charge. Then Gudarz turned suddenly to his grandson Bizhān, saying, 'Sadly do we miss the Banner of Kāva beneath which Persians have ever fought since the days of good King Feridun. Ride swiftly after Feriburz and fetch it. With the Banner flying above us we shall be mightily heartened and do great deeds here, I promise you.'

So, while his few brave comrades remained to face Pirān's onslaught, Bizhān, spurring on his horse, rode like the wind after the retreating army. When he came up with Feriburz and the men who rode about the Banner, he said, 'Lord commander, come back to those of us who still fight, and bring with you the Banner of Kāva. With you to lead us, and the Banner to inspire us, we may yet win the day. Or, if you will not come yourself, then give me the Banner and I will carry it to Gudarz and to my father.'

But Feriburz answered him, 'Go, return to a hopeless fight if you will. But I am not yet crazed enough by sorrow for this day's defeat, to follow you and stand with Giv and Gudarz to win only certain death. As for the Banner of Kāva, the Great King Khosroes gave me the charge of his army, and I am thus the protector of the Banner. It shall not leave my side.'

At that, Bizhān, on an impulse, drew his sword, and pressing his horse forward, he slashed the Banner in two along its length. Then, seizing one half, he turned his horse and rode back to where the battle, once again, was raging. When they saw the Banner, mutilated though it was, the Persians who fought beside Giv and Gudarz raised a shout. Fresh strength came to their tired limbs and new hope to their weary hearts, and they fought once again as though they were only that very moment come to battle.

From the Turanian ranks the general Humān—who was brother to Pirān—said, 'See, our enemy rallies once more about the Banner of Kāva. If we could capture that Banner which they prize so highly, I have no doubt but that our victory would follow swiftly.'

They attacked then fiercely and furiously, but were driven off time after time by Giv and Gudarz and Bizhān. Yet so outnumbered were the Persians that, little by little, they were forced to retreat towards the mountains and their camp; and when darkness fell, though that half of the Banner about which they fought was yet uncaptured, and though Giv and Gudarz and Bizhān and several of their valiant comrades still lived, the day had, without doubt, brought victory to the rejoicing army of Turān; and, once back in their own camp, the Turanians celebrated with song and feasting.

Feriburz, with his remaining generals and men, led the broken army of Persia towards the borderlands; and so, after some days, they reached Persia and safety and brought their ill tidings to Khosroes, who grieved greatly for the loss of so many brave warriors. Blaming those who had led the army, he took from all his generals their honours and rank, banishing them from his presence with angry words.

In Turān it was far otherwise. When Pirān brought back his men to Afrāsib to report that no single living man of all the great Persian army now remained on Turanian ground, the crowds pressed about him as he rode in triumph to the imperial palace, showering him with gold and flowers, and shouting out their praises of him from rooftops spread with coloured cloths, while bright streamers and green branches waved everywhere.

For two weeks Afrāsib and his court rejoiced with music and feasting and entertained Pirān, for whom—since it seemed that Ormuzd favoured him—no reward seemed too great. Then, with his own band of troops, Pirān rode for his own home, the province of Khotān, hoping to pass his remaining days there in peace—if peace were granted him—yet knowing that he must ever hold himself in readiness once more to lead the Turanian army at Afrāsib's command, should war arise again and Khosroes seek to avenge his present defeat.

17: Rustem's Battle with Pulādvend

AFTER the humiliation of the Persian generals, the imperial army, lacking leaders, remained idle; and so, for a brief space, there was peace between Khosroes and Afrāsib and their two great empires. Then Rustem, thinking it a shame that the Persian defeat should go unavenged, came from Zābulestān to the capital to urge that the Great King should once more send his men against Turān. Khosroes, who had been fretting himself at the idleness of his army, would have given Rustem charge of it; but though he was by far the greatest warrior in Persia—and, indeed, in all the world—Rustem's great joy in battle was in single combat against the best and strongest and most skilled antagonists who could be sent against him, and in fighting large numbers of foemen at one time. He was no willing leader of great armies, preferring to lead only his own small band of brave warriors from Zābulestān. And he cared little for the deployment of troops and the contrivance of cunning stratagems, preferring to leave these matters to others, while he went about the business of slaying enemies with his own hands.

Rustem pleaded with Khosroes for the generals who had been degraded; and at length Khosroes was persuaded by his arguments and, relenting, summoned the generals to him once more and restored to them—even to the inept Tus, who had regained his reason in the seclusion of his home—their positions of trust and command. Once again the Persian army and its generals and champions set forth against Turān; and this time, to their great comfort, Rustem rode with them, on Raksh.

Pirān, recalled from Khotān by Afrāsib at the moment of learning that the Persians were on the march, came once again into the field at the head of the Turanians; and this time, expecting another easy victory, Afrāsib rode in great pomp beside him. At first, with forays and skirmishing, with attack and retreat and retreat and attack, neither side had the advantage. Then Rustem took up his huge bow and his quiver of long arrows and began to shoot. Every arrow found its mark and a Turanian warrior fell, never to rise again. The Turanians, marvelling, examined these arrows carefully. 'Each is the length and weight of a spear,' they said. 'Who can be strong enough to bend a bow which shoots such arrows as these?' And then word went round among them, 'It is great Rustem himself who has come against us,' and a shiver of apprehension ran through the Turanian ranks.

Not only with his death-bearing arrows did Rustem bring doom to the Turanians; many of Afrāsib's finest champions he slew in single combat, while the men of both armies stood by and looked on, the Persians with delight and rejoicing, and the Turanians with ever-increasing distress. But one of these combats, because of the treachery of Afrāsib, came very near to ending Rustem's life.

Among the Turanian champions there was a certain foreign warrior named Pulādvend, a huge man, as broad and tall as Rustem and of immense strength; who, alone and at one time, had worsted and wounded the whole family of Gudarz. This Pulādvend and Rustem met first on horseback, after Pulādvend had slain several Persian champions. Rustem, seeing the other's height and breadth and sinewy limbs, thought that here, at last, was an opponent worthy of him, could they stand face to face unarmed and try their strength in a bout of wrestling. His challenge was accepted, and when it had been agreed to by both Tus and Afrāsib, Rustem and Pulādvend cast aside sword and spear and bow and dismounted eagerly, stripping off their armoured jackets and their upper garments. The two armies paused to watch, drawn up in their ranks, and the generals and leaders of both sides stepped closer to see them better; Tus and Giv and Gudarz and their fellow-leaders upon one side of the space marked out for the wrestling; and on the other, the Turanian generals with Pirān, Afrāsib and Afrāsib's son, Shida.

The opponents touched hands briefly and warily circled about each other; then both in the same moment closed rapidly in, snatching at the other's belt and drawing him closer; then they caught each other about the middle in a grip that would have crushed the bones of any man of ordinary build or strength. Roaring like lions, they wrestled for hours, each trying, first with one clever grip and then with another, to throw his opponent to the ground. The hot sun shone down upon them and their bodies glistened and grew slippery with sweat, so that each grip became more difficult to hold than the last, as they strained every mighty muscle. Yet, so strong and so worthy an adversary for Rustem was Pulādvend, that for a long time neither had the advantage. Then, at last, Pulādvend began to tire. He came in to the attack less frequently, and he was forced more and more to defend himself against Rustem's moves.

Afrāsib saw this with dismay, for at the outset of the match he had had great hope that his champion might be the victor and, by crippling—or perhaps by slaying, even—their most feared and dangerous enemy, bring great encouragement to the Turanian cause. In their belts Rustem and Pulādvend still wore the only weapons which they had not laid aside, the short daggers with which the victor might dispatch the loser; and the sight of these daggers suddenly brought hope back to Afrāsib's heart. Turning to his son Shida, who sat his horse at his father's side, Afrāsib said in a low voice, 'Go closer to them, under pretence of wishing to see the better, and tell Pulādvend, in his own tongue, to use his dagger on Rustem now. That way, we may be sure of his victory.'

Shida, outraged, exclaimed, 'That would be black treachery and unworthy of an emperor, my father. You gave your royal word that the two should wrestle unarmed.'

'What of it?' demanded Afrāsib angrily. 'At all costs we must rid ourselves of Rustem. We would be fools indeed not to take the chance which is offered us while it is there. We may never again see Rustem unarmed.'

When Shida protested further, Afrāsib said, 'One who is so sorry a warrior as you, my son, has no right to offer counsel in the matter of war and battles. The only weapons, Shida, with which you have any skill, are ill-considered words. Do as I bid you.'

And when Shida still sought to urge his father against so dishonourable a course, Afrāsib cursed him for an undutiful son, who wished in his heart for a Persian victory, and who desired only to see his father cast down from his throne, that he himself might take his place and make alliance with his country's enemies. 'If you will not do as I command you,' he finished furiously, 'then I must act myself.' Raging inside himself, he moved his horse nearer to Rustem and Pulādvend and leaned forward over the horse's neck as though, in his great interest and admiration, he would have watched the wrestlers more closely. Then, when he saw an opportunity, he called out to Pulādvend in the champion's own tongue, 'Good Pulādvend, you wish to be the victor, do you not? As soon as you may safely do so, draw your dagger and stab our enemy to the heart. It is your duty as my champion to act thus. All Turān will honour you for the deed.'

Rustem heard Afrāsib speak, but not understanding the tongue, he thought the words to be spoken merely in encouragement. But fortunately Giv, who stood the nearest of the Persian generals, caught them. He understood the language of Pulādvend's country, and so knew what Afrāsib had demanded of his champion. Appalled, he moved closer to the struggling antagonists and said urgently to Rustem, 'Take care! Afrāsib has bidden Pulādvend use his dagger on you. For the love of Ormuzd, watch him well.'

Rustem gave an angry roar; then, calling out to Giv, 'Have no fear for me, my friend,' he exerted all his strength—now increased by rage at the knowledge of Afrāsib's treachery—and clasping Pulādvend about the neck with both his hands in an unbreakable grip, he raised him and swung him up above his head, around and around, then dashed him to the ground. There Pulādvend lay, unable to rise; and so Afrāsib's treachery had come to naught.

The Persians, mightily encouraged, raised a cheer for Rustem which echoed all around; they blew their trumpets and stamped and sounded their drums; while Shida gave a sigh of relief that his father had been spared the shame which he had risked. As for Pulādvend, when he was able to rise again, he departed from the battlefield and returned to his own distant land, and he troubled the Persians no more.

Indeed, so enheartened were the Persians by Rustem's victory over Pulādvend, and so dismayed the Turanians seemed to them by the worsting of their most powerful champion, that, on Rustem's urging, Tus and Gudarz ordered the Persians to attack immediately with a rain of arrows, before their enemies had time to recover their spirits. It was done, and that day the Persians won a great victory. The warriors of Turān were routed, and the Emperor Afrāsib fled for his life from the battlefield. And so, with Rustem escorted in triumph, the Persian army returned to the Great King Khosroes with the glad tidings that their former defeat had been avenged in full.

18: Rustem and Akvān the Demon

ONE morning when Khosroes was in his throne-room, giving audience to any who sought the justice of the Great King, and King of Kings, or his decision in any matter, a horse-dealer came before him, and kneeling down, implored his help. This man had of late moved his herd to new pastureland, near to a certain spring. The grazing there was good, but, as he said, a huge wild ass, of ferocious and hideous aspect, had come among his herd and now ran with it and could not be driven away. 'It is a terrible beast, Great King,' said the man. 'It fights and wounds the stallions, it terrifies the mares and savages the foals, so that I lose a fine, promising colt or filly every day. And several times it has stampeded the whole herd, so that I and my men have had great pains in rounding up the horses and, indeed, several of them we have lost, for in their terror they have fallen with broken legs or backs, while others have fled away and not been seen again. With each day that passes, Great King, it seems as though this wild ass becomes stronger and fiercer. And now my men no longer dare approach it to drive it away, for, three days past, it killed two of them, trampling them into the dust. If we seek to shoot it from a distance, however true our aim, we always find that our arrows have gone wide of their mark, or that, instead of this monster ass—which seems to us all to be blessed and preserved by Ahrimān—we have slain one of our finest horses, though it stood a hundred paces or more away from our target. I beg of you, Great King, send some brave warrior to slay this beast, before I lose every horse in my herd.'

'This seems to me to be no wild ass, but a demon in ass's shape,' said Khosroes. He questioned the horse-dealer further, and then he questioned the older men among his courtiers concerning the place where the herd was pastured, and several among them remembered hearing formerly old tales of a demon named Akvān which dwelt in the spring at this spot. 'It would surely be that evil fiend which is bent on destroying the herd of this unfortunate man,' they said.

'That is as I guessed,' said Khosroes. Then to the horse-dealer he gave his word that he would send a warrior to destroy the demon. But when he called for one of his champions or his courtiers to undertake the deed, where, a bare hour before, they had been idle, he now found them all to be busied with other tasks and duties, and regretfully unable to spare the time for demon-slaying.

'I had not until this moment known that in my court I have none but faint-hearted boys and feeble women,' said Khosroes. 'Were Rustem here today, I would not have to ask twice for a demon-slayer.' And he sent a speedy messenger to Rustem, bidding him come to the capital with no delay.

As soon as he had the Great King's message, Rustem rode from his palace in Zābul; and when he learnt from Khosroes what was required of him, he laughed gleefully and said, 'This is a task such as ever pleases me best. Be this monster a wild ass, a demon, or Ahrimān himself, I will rid the world of it.' And guided by the horse-dealer, he set off at once.

Arriving at the grazing-ground, for three days Rustem searched the pleasant countryside about the spring for a sight of Akvān, yet without success. And then, on the fourth day, he saw a wild ass galloping among the horses. It was indeed a huge beast, rust-coloured and hideous, for ever biting a horse here and kicking another there, and braying all the time fit to terrify the rest.

'A monster truly,' said Rustem to the drovers. 'I shall catch it and carry it alive to the Great King, for he will marvel much at it.' But when he had ridden close enough to the beast and had taken in his hands and swung above his head a noosed rope which he would have cast about its neck, the wild ass suddenly vanished from sight without moving a step from the spot where Rustem had been watching it. 'This will truly be Akvān, the demon of the spring,' he thought. 'And that being so, I had best slay him here, in this place, for it would be rash indeed to capture a demon alive.' He fitted an arrow to his bow and looked about him keenly, his eyes narrowed against the bright sunlight; but he saw around him only the horses of the herd; of Akvān there was no sight. And then, after a minute or so, as suddenly as it had vanished, the wild ass appeared again. Rustem loosed his bow instantly and rode towards the demon-beast; but, unerring as had been his aim, his arrow did not find its mark because, once again, the wild ass had disappeared from sight. Soon after, it reappeared a short distance away; but once more, as soon as Rustem shot an arrow, it was gone, only to return to sight a little farther on. In this manner Rustem pursued it vainly for a whole day, and for the space of a moonlit night as well, until he and Raksh were wearied from the fruitless chase and far from Akvān's spring. Then, at dawning the next day, when Rustem felt as though if he rode but another half league more, he would fall asleep in the saddle, he saw before him a pleasant shady well, where he and Raksh might rest awhile and drink. At that moment there was no sign of the wild ass, only its tracks leading onward, so Rustem dismounted. When both he and Raksh had drunk their fill, taking his saddle covered by its leopard-skin saddle-cloth for a pillow, and with his drawn sword close at hand, Rustem lay down to sleep, while Raksh, near by, slept also.

As soon as Akvān the demon saw that he was no longer being followed, he changed himself from a wild ass into a rushing wind and, returning to the place where Rustem and Raksh were lying, he blew silently at the ground in a circle about Rustem, digging a trench in the earth with his breath. Then, burrowing under the ground, he lifted up the disc of earth upon which Rustem lay and bore it high into the air.

Rustem awoke to find himself being swept along at a dizzy height above the ground by a mighty, rushing wind; and realizing at once what must have happened, he cursed his folly in allowing himself to rest and sleep before he had destroyed the demon.

As soon as he saw that Rustem was awake, Akvān gave an evil chuckle and said, 'Good day to you, elephant among men. Are you now awoken from your sleep? Truly, you have slept soundly, Rustem, and I can promise you that soon you will be sleeping even more soundly.' He laughed again. 'You sought me out only to slay me and for no other purpose, which was no friendly act. Yet I am fair-minded, Rustem, and I am willing to leave the choice to you: shall I cast you down on to the mountains, or into the sea? Which do you fancy, to break in little pieces on the rocks and be eaten by wild beasts, or to drown in the salt sea and be nibbled by fishes? Speak, and you shall have your choice.'

But Rustem did not trust the demon, and for a minute or so he considered the matter and at length he guessed that Akvān meant to deal out to him that fate which was the one he did not choose. So, believing that only certain death could be his fate, were he dropped on to the sharp rocks of a mountain; but that, in the sea, he might have a chance to save his life; he said, 'It would be a sorry fate for one who has ever tried to live as a brave warrior should, to end in the gut of a timid fish. Better by far to fill the maw of a noble lion or a fierce leopard. Therefore, I beg you, drop me on the mountains.'

Akvān gave a roar of laughter like the howling of a storm. 'You shall go where you will be lost to men for ever,' he shrieked. 'No man shall see you again from now until the end of time.' And with a blast like a hurricane he blew Rustem through the sky until he was above the ocean, and there he dropped him. Down, down fell Rustem through the air, down to the cold grey sea. Then down, down through the water he plunged; until at last he touched bottom and then slowly—how slowly—he fought his way upwards to the surface and came, gasping and heaving for breath, once more into the air and the light of day. And above the sound of his own struggles, he could hear the evil laughter of Akvān dying away on the rushing wind.

From the sun in the sky, Rustem judged where the nearest land must lie, and with his sword in his hand, ready to fight off the attacks of sharks and sea-creatures, he swam in that direction. After what seemed like many hours, he saw land before his eyes, there, where he had judged it to be. The sight gave his weary limbs new power and he swam on more hopefully. At last he reached the shore and dragged himself beyond the reach of the waves on to the sandy beach, and lay there almost like one dead.

When he had recovered his strength, he stood up and looked about him and saw to his satisfaction that he was not too far from the shady well where he had rested in his chase after the demon. As swiftly as he could, he made his way to the place. There lay his armour where he had put it off, and there lay Raksh's saddle; but of Raksh himself, there was no sign. Supposing Raksh to have wandered off in search of him, Rustem looked about him for hoofprints, and sure enough, he found them, leading away from the well. He followed the tracks, calling to Raksh as he went; but in vain, for there came no answering whinny. Then, after several hours, when he had lost the hoofprints on stony ground, from the top of a low hill he looked down into a green valley and saw a herd of horses. 'There among his own kind, Raksh may well be,' he thought, and strode down towards the herd.

But, unknown to him, in his search for Raksh he had wandered over the borderlands and on to Turanian soil. The first he knew of it was when he came upon a mare that cropped the grass a little apart from the rest of the herd and saw on her quarters the imperial brand of Turān. 'Aha!' he said to himself, well pleased at the sight. 'If Raksh is indeed here, between the two of us we will take home some booty.'

After that he went more warily, lest any watchful drover spied him; and then he waited, concealed, until such time as he judged the drovers would be together in one spot, sheltering from the high, noontide sun and eating their midday meal. When he left his hiding-place, this was, indeed, how he found them, beside a stream in the shadow of a spreading tree, some of the men eating and drinking, some lying asleep, and others chatting idly while they rested. And then, at last, Rustem saw Raksh, feeding among the herd. He could not call to Raksh without the drovers hearing him; so, approaching as close as he could without too much risk, he took the noosed rope with which he had hoped to snare Akvān, and swinging it high above his head, he cast it with true aim around the neck of Raksh and pulled it tight. Plunging and rearing, Raksh resisted; but with his great strength Rustem dragged the big horse towards him until Raksh saw who his captor was, grew calm in a moment, and with a whinny of pleasure, trotted towards Rustem.

With Raksh saddled and bridled once more and Rustem mounted on his back, all was ready for the horse-raiding. Slowly and quietly Rustem rode in narrowing circles around the herd, until the mares and their foals were bunched together; then calling to them and lashing out with his rope, he began to drive them away. The drowsy drovers heard his cries, the sound of his slapping rope and the disturbed neighing of the herd, and jumped to their feet. Shouting, some of them ran after Rustem, while others took up their bows and shot at his back. Their arrows missed. Rustem drew his sword, turned Raksh speedily, and shouting out, 'I am Rustem, son of Zāl!' he struck down the nearest of them. The others took fright and fled for their lives, leaving Rustem with his booty. Chuckling to himself at the thought of Afrāsib's anger when he learnt of his loss, Rustem drove the stolen horses towards Akvān's spring and there gave them into the charge of the astonished Persian drovers. Then, his score with Akvān still to be settled, he concealed himself and Raksh beside the spring to wait, hidden, until such time as Akvān should once more appear in his wild ass shape to disport himself in his wonted manner.

Sure enough, before many hours had passed, the monster ass showed itself. Taking Akvān, who believed him drowned, quite by surprise, Rustem cast his noosed rope about his neck and pulled it tight. As Akvān changed to his own demon shape and put his hands to his throat to loosen the rope, Rustem urged Raksh forward at a gallop from behind the undergrowth where they had lain concealed, and in a moment was at the demon's side. Before Akvān had even the brief time he needed to make himself invisible, and so escape, Rustem had struck him down with his sword.

As he fell, Akvān saw Rustem, triumphant, towering above him. 'Have you returned alive from the sea to be slain by me once more?' he bellowed threateningly. But they were the last words he spoke, for Rustem, dismounting, hacked his head from his body and so made an end of Akvān, the demon of the spring. Never again were the horse-drovers plagued and molested when they pastured their herds in that place.

19: Bizhān and Manizha

ONE year, in the forestland of the province of Armān, near the Turanian border, there appeared a large herd of wild boar, too many for the hunters of Armān to slay unaided, and which, unchecked, did much damage to the crops. In despair the farmers of Armān appealed to the Great King Khosroes, asking that he would send a skilled hunter to destroy the boars and save what remained of their harvest.

'Who will go to Armān and rid the province of this plague?' asked Khosroes of his courtiers.

Immediately, before any other could reply, the son of Giv, young Bizhān, who had led the final assault against King Forud of Kalāt, leapt to his feet excitedly, exclaiming, 'By your leave, Great King, I will go.'

Khosroes was pleased by his eagerness, and Bizhān made ready at once to set out with his followers for Armān.

From childhood on, Bizhān had had a friend, Gorgin, his inferior in rank and fighting-skill, who had been his companion in several adventures and his comrade in several battles; Gorgin's exploits, both in peace and war, being ever outshone by Bizhān's. Over the years Bizhān had come to take Gorgin's affection and loyalty for granted, and to be high-handed in all his dealings with his friend; and he had never noticed how, little by little, Gorgin's love had changed to envy and his loyalty to resentment.

Carelessly, Bizhān now bade Gorgin go with him to Armān to hunt boar, never thinking to ask him whether that was his wish or not. They set out together with their followers, Bizhān gay and eager and Gorgin hardly able to master his bitterness and keep his jealousy hidden. Because Bizhān desired it, they journeyed slowly towards Armān, hunting and hawking as they went, and having much good sport.

On their arrival in Armān the farmers led them to the outskirts of that stretch of forestland, extending over the border country and into Turān, where the wild boar had their retreat and from whence they came in scores to raid the cultivated fields and devour the crops. Bizhān sent his followers into the woods to flush the game, proposing to station himself on the edge of the cleared land with his bow and shoot the boar as they were driven out into the open.

'Do you,' he said to Gorgin, 'stand in the fields a little way off, at my back, with your axe, and strike down any boar that escape my arrows.'

His usual careless arrogance and presumption were too much for Gorgin. The years'-long hidden resentment broke loose and his envy showed itself at last. 'I will do no such thing!' he exclaimed. 'Is it not enough that I have come with you on this undertaking, for which all the glory—and any reward—will be yours alone? Must I, as ever, give you my help unthanked and unacknowledged? I am weary of standing in your shadow. As yours will be the credit for the slaying of the boar, so also can yours be the labour of it.' And Gorgin turned and walked away.

Astonished, Bizhān stared after his friend, never before having heard him speak so. But such was Bizhān's lack of understanding and his selfishness, he never dreamt that he himself might be at fault in any way, or that it was his treatment of Gorgin which had brought about his outburst. He presumed that his friend must be unwell and unwilling to admit it, or that someone else had angered him, or that he was troubled at heart about some matter or another. 'As you will,' he said, shrugging his shoulders. 'As you will.' And he turned his mind to the boar, thinking no more of Gorgin's unwonted mood.

Had Bizhān shown only a little understanding of his friend's grievance; and had he, even then, before it was too late, called to Gorgin to come back and stand at his side because his help was needed, then Bizhān would have been spared the trials that were to fall on him and the pains he was to suffer.

As it was, Gorgin walked away injured, angry, and swearing to himself that Bizhān should pay for his arrogance and thoughtlessness. He mounted his horse and rode off at a furious gallop, spurring the poor beast through the forestland towards the Turanian border, paying little attention to where he went. When he at last reined in the exhausted horse and looked about him, he recognized a region where he had on occasion hunted in the company of Giv and Gudarz—the fact that their hunting had been on Turanian soil having added a seasoning of danger to increase their pleasure in the chase. And he remembered also that, not more than a day's journey away, there stretched a woodland glade, a place of great beauty, with a stream and shady trees and flowers of every kind and singing birds, where the ladies of the Turanian imperial court often set up their pavilions during the days of summer heat, that they might enjoy the fresh, cool breezes and the sounds and sights of the woodland. An idea for vengeance came into Gorgin's mind and he smiled to himself, turned his horse's head and rode back to Bizhān.

The hunt had been more than successful. Score after score of wild boar had been slain; the farmers were ungrudging with their thanks and praise; and Bizhān had enjoyed himself. Amid the bustle of pavilions being set up for the night, and boar's flesh being roasted for the evening meal, Gorgin met his friend with smiles and congratulations.

Bizhān had completely forgotten Gorgin's strange mood of that morning. He smiled at him in return. 'Tonight we remain here,' he said. 'Tomorrow we leave for home.'

'Why do we leave so soon?' asked Gorgin. 'I can show you spoils with which to ride home of far more worth than a few boars' tusks and the tale of a successful hunt.'

'What spoils are those?'

'I know the countryside about this place,' said Gorgin. 'I have been here before. A few leagues on lies Turān and less than two days' journey from here there is a pleasant glade where the ladies of Afrāsib's court often set up their pavilions in the summer days. Why should we not ride home with a few Turanian captives? Afrāsib would no doubt pay a good ransom for their safe return; and if not, why then, we shall have gained for ourselves a pretty slave or two. Either way we are the winners. What say you to it, Bizhān, shall we try our luck?'

'A pleasing jest for us to play on Afrāsib,' laughed Bizhān. 'You shall show me these fair Turanians and I will plan our raiding.'

At dawn they set off under Gorgin's direction, and by the evening they were a bare league or two from the forest clearing which was their goal. Bizhān and Gorgin and their followers set up pavilions for the night; and in the morning, at Gorgin's suggestion, the two young men rode off alone to spy upon the Turanians. From the shelter of a group of trees, Bizhān and Gorgin were able to overlook their pavilions and watch the ladies as they sat beside the stream or picked the sweet flowers which grew everywhere. One pavilion was larger and finer than the others, and from the imperial emblems on it, they guessed it to belong to one of the wives or daughters of Afrāsib, and they made merry over the thought of Afrāsib's anger at being forced to ransom her.

Gorgin had not been sure of how he would accomplish his betrayal of his friend into Turanian hands, but Bizhān made all easy for him by of a sudden yawning and saying, 'I grow sleepy and I shall rest an hour or two before we ride back. What better place to rest than here, so close to so much beauty! Do you keep watch and rouse me if any Turanian guards approach.' He lay down amidst the fallen blossoms below a flowering tree and soon was fast asleep.

Gorgin waited for a time while Bizhān slept and then, to his satisfaction, he saw a group of maidens walking near by and with each step approaching closer to the young men's hiding-place. They were gathering armfuls of flowers; and there was among them some lady of obvious high station and importance. Smiling to himself, Gorgin made a disturbance among the trees, and as soon as he was certain that they had heard him, he mounted his horse and rode off at a good pace.

But things did not go quite as Gorgin had intended, for when the startled girls heard the sounds he made and looked to their mistress to tell them what they should do, she did not, as Gorgin had expected, send one of them running for a guard to seek out the cause of the disturbance; instead she said, 'It will most likely be no more than a horse or a baggage ass, broken from its tether.' And she sent two of the girls to look among the trees. They returned, breathless and very excited, to say that they had found a young warrior lying asleep beneath a tree, richly clad and, from his garments, a Persian.

Their mistress considered a moment and then she said, 'I have never seen a Persian warrior, young or old, sleeping or awake. There could be no harm in my looking at him before we call the guards to take him captive.' So, bidding the two girls lead the way, she followed them to where Bizhān lay. And the moment that she saw him lying there, so young and handsome, asleep and helpless, straightway she loved him as she had never thought it possible to love. She did not call the guards; instead she dissembled and said, 'That is no Persian. No enemy could look so good and gentle; and no enemy, alone and unguarded, would dare to sleep as soundly, so close to our pavilions. He will most certainly be one of my father's warriors who has ridden out hunting and now rests here to escape the midday sun. Let us leave him to enjoy his slumber.' When she and the two girls had rejoined the others, she said, 'Now I, too, would rest. Let us return to my pavilion.' But, once there, she secretly sent her old nurse to greet Bizhān from her and ask his name. 'For,' she said, 'he seems to me to be no ordinary mortal man, but a good spirit sent by Ormuzd; or perhaps dead Siyāvush, that pattern of Persian manhood, who wed my eldest sister in the years before I was born, Siyāvush of whom I have heard so many tales, come back to life to bless our land of Turān with his presence once again.'

Bizhān awoke to see, not Gorgin beside him, but a woman of middle years who said to him, 'My mistress, the Princess Manizha, youngest daughter of the Emperor Afrāsib, sends to you her greetings and asks your name. She says that surely you must be a good spirit, or else Siyāvush returned to grace Turān.'

Bizhān, flattered and well pleased, blushed a little at these compliments and answered them with compliments of his own. 'Indeed,' he said, 'I am no heavenly spirit, nor am I Siyāvush returned to life. I am Bizhān, son of Giv, and grandson of famed Gudarz. Greet your mistress from me in return and tell her that I have been hunting in the forest, and that, hearing of her great beauty, I came to this place in the hope that I might catch a glimpse of her.'

The nurse returned to Manizha with his message. Manizha was overjoyed. 'Dear nurse, go back to him and tell him that he may indeed see me. Say that he will be welcome in my pavilion as an honoured guest. But warn him that, as a Persian, he must not come among us openly, but secretly and after dusk.'

Bizhān, who had, for a brief space, wondered why Gorgin was no longer at his side, forgot his friend entirely when he had Manizha's second message. He waited eagerly for the evening and the return of the nurse, to lead him to her mistress.

When Bizhān and Manizha stood face to face, it was with him as it had been with her, and he loved her from that moment. They wept a little together, because they were enemies and no open marriage between them would be possible; but mostly they smiled at one another and were happy in each other's company. For three days Bizhān remained with Manizha, hidden in her pavilion with only the nurse and her most trusted slave-girls knowing her secret. But on the fourth day it was time for Manizha to return to the imperial palace in the capital, and she dared delay no longer lest questions be asked.

Her distress at their parting was pitiful. 'Yet there is no help for it. I must leave you, even though we may never meet again,' said Bizhān.

But Manizha could not give him up, now that she had found him and now that she knew that she would love him for ever. In her desperation a reckless plan formed in her mind. She dried her tears and said, 'If we must part, beloved, let us drink one last cup of wine together.'

The wine was poured and, unknown to Bizhān, Manizha dropped into his cup a draught which would make him sleep soundly for many hours. When he was asleep she had him laid in her palanquin and spread over with a coverlet. Then she took her place beside him and gave the order for the cavalcade to move. And thus, sleeping and in all ignorance, Bizhān entered the palace of Afrāsib.

When he awoke and knew that he was in Manizha's apartments in the women's quarters in the innermost rooms of the palace of the Emperor of Turān, Bizhān was appalled, remembering the tales told in Persia of the fate of Siyāvush, who had wed Afrāsib's eldest daughter—tales which Manizha had not heard, since they were not repeated in the palace of Afrāsib.

'If Afrāsib cut the throat of Siyāvush, Siyāvush to whom he had himself given his daughter as a wife, what hope have I of escaping death, I who have taken his daughter unbidden?' Bizhān asked.

'Perchance my father may never learn of our love,' said Manizha, though she was beginning to tremble at the thought of the consequences of her rash deed.

'How can our secret be kept for ever?' said Bizhān. 'Already too many of your women know of it.'

'When he learns how much I love you, and how strong is your love for me, perhaps he will forgive us,' said Manizha, as though by saying the impossible words, she might make them true.

'He will not forgive us,' Bizhān replied.

'Then let us be happy and rejoice in our love while we may, whether it is fated to end in shameful death or in honourable marriage,' said Manizha. And she ordered the choicest delicacies and the best of wines to be set before them; and sent for musicians and dancers for their entertainment.

And so they passed their days in a wild joy which was all the sweeter because they both knew that it might well be short-lived; for, in their hearts, they both knew that they had no hope at all of mercy from Afrāsib.

Soon rumours of strange doings in the apartments of the Princess Manizha came to the ears of Afrāsib's chamberlain, and he dared not ignore them lest he brought his master's anger on his own head. He made what inquiries he might, was appalled at what he was told; and then went to Afrāsib and repeated the tales that were being whispered about his daughter.

Afrāsib, scowling, sent for his brother Garsivāz and bade him go to Manizha's apartments to see for himself the truth of the rumours. 'And be sure that you enter unannounced and take her by surprise,' he demanded. 'And before you enter, see that you have armed men at every door, so that this intruder—if there is indeed one—may not escape.'

So Garsivāz posted guards at every door to the women's quarters and upon the roof also; then, with his sword drawn and in his hand, and armed men at his back, he entered Manizha's apartments, where no sound of his coming had reached by reason of the music of flute and harp and timbrel and the sweet singing with which Manizha and Bizhān were being diverted.

They were taken quite unawares, Bizhān with a wine-cup in one hand and his arm about Manizha, and with no weapon save a small dagger at his belt. The musicians ceased their playing and the dancers fled, only to be caught at every door by Garsivāz's men. Deploring that he had neither sword nor horse when both were so much needed, Bizhān rose and set himself before Manizha, his little dagger in his hand. Above the terrified screaming of Manizha's women, he called to Garsivāz, 'I am Bizhān, son of Giv, grandson of Gudarz, and in birth I am the equal of any Turanian lord. I am, moreover, the equal of any Turanian warrior, as your men will learn to their cost, if they lay their hands on me, though I have but a dagger with which to defend myself. Yet it is not fighting and slaughter that I would choose. Rather, take me to the Emperor Afrāsib, that I may speak for myself and ask his mercy.'

'You shall have all honourable treatment, as befits a nobleman and a respected warrior, and you shall speak freely to the Emperor in your defence. Yet give up your dagger, for it is not fitting that a suppliant should go armed into the Emperor's presence.'

Thus, with lying promises Garsivāz won Bizhān's dagger from him; and, that being done, he had Bizhān bound with strong cords, so that he could move neither hand nor foot. Then, in this sorry plight, Bizhān was dragged into the presence of Afrāsib and flung to the floor at the foot of the Emperor's throne.

'It is ill enough for a father that he should have an unchaste daughter who presumes it her right to take a husband of her own choosing,' said Afrāsib. 'But that she should choose one of her country's enemies, has put her beyond the reach of any forgiveness of mine. You shall both die for it, and as shamefully as you deserve.'

'At least grant me the death of a warrior,' pleaded Bizhān. 'Give me a horse and a battle-mace, then set against me a thousand of your men and I shall show you how a Persian warrior fights and dies.'

'You shall have the death you deserve, and thus all men shall be warned by your fate,' said Afrāsib. And he ordered a high gallows to be set up outside the city gates, and Bizhān to be hanged there in chains, alive, to die slowly in the sight of all who passed through the gates, as a reminder to them of the Emperor's wrath. It was done as Afrāsib had commanded; and when the gallows was raised Bizhān was fetched from prison and his guards made ready to carry out to the end their Emperor's orders.

Now, it happened that at that time Pirān had left his kingdom of Khotān to travel to the imperial court, and at the very moment when the guards were hoisting Bizhān, in chains, to the top of the gallows, the old commander-in-chief came by. He asked the name and offence of the young prisoner, and on learning both, bade the guards stay their hands until he had seen Afrāsib and pleaded for Bizhān's life.

At first Afrāsib would not listen to Pirān, though the old man reminded him that, at that particular time, matters were peaceable enough between the two empires, Persia and Turān. 'But,' he said, 'when they learn in Persia that you have slain the grandson of the famed general and warrior Gudarz—and only for the crime of loving your daughter—the Great King Khosroes will send his army and all his champions—and Rustem among them, no doubt—to take vengeance for Bizhān's shameful death.'

'Would you have me, through fear of war, pardon one who has crept like a thief into my palace and stolen my daughter? Though you seem to care little for my good name, Pirān, I have no wish to be a laughing-stock to every man in the two empires.'

Seeing that he could not win Afrāsib's mercy, Pirān said, 'To one of Bizhan's youth and courage, death—any death—would seem better than a life of misery and torment. Spare Bizhan's life, lord Emperor, but let him live it out alone and in prison. That fate would serve as a warning to others as much as would his death upon the gallows.' Thus Pirān advised, because he knew that, so long as a man had life—even if he lived in a cage—so long was there hope of his eventual freedom. And when Afrāsib's first anger was past, he thought, the Emperor might one day be induced to free Bizhān.

There was a long silence after Pirān had spoken; then, 'Let it be as you ask,' said Afrāsib. And he had Bizhān, still in chains, flung into a deep, dark pit, and over the top of the pit a large stone slab was laid, cutting off the blessing of the sun and leaving only a narrow crack through which a thin blade of light could creep, to make the black night of imprisonment seem even darker.

'As for Manizha,' said Afrāsib, 'she is no longer any child of mine.' And he ordered her to be stripped of her jewels and her royal robes and taken to the place where Bizhān lay in his pit.

'Let her see and lament her lover's fate and pass her days in weeping,' he said. 'She may wander where she will and beg her bread. And on the heads of any who aid her, shall my displeasure fall.'

Manizha lay on the stony ground and, with tears, called down to Bizhān; and with tears and in desperation he called back to her. Until her nails were broken and her fingers bleeding, she clawed and scrabbled vainly at the stone which it had taken many strong men to set in place. Day after day she remained above Bizhān's living tomb and did not wander far away save to find what food she could by begging or by stealing. Few dared to pity her for fear of the Emperor's wrath and none dared give her aid for fear of punishment. Each day she shared with Bizhān the poor crusts and crumbs she gathered, dropping them down through the crack to him. And so the days passed for them in misery and sorrow until, thin, haggard, and dishevelled, no one who had looked upon her face in the old, happy days, would have known poor Manizha for the Emperor's once lovely daughter.

After Manizha and her retinue had left the forest clearing where she and Bizhān had found each other, Gorgin had returned to the spot alone, almost hoping to find Bizhān there, safe and unharmed; for he had been beginning to repent of his deed. But, by that time, Bizhān had been in Afrāsib's palace with Manizha, celebrating their love with music and feasting; so Gorgin, having given Bizhān's followers some lying tale to explain their master's absence, had ridden home with them, bearing the tusks of the slain boar. To Bizhān's father, Giv, Gorgin said that Bizhān had gone alone in pursuit of a particularly large boar and been lost. But his manner seemed to Giv to be fearful and guilty, and he dragged Gorgin to the palace and accused him before Khosroes of treachery and falsehood. Gorgin, by then remorseful and wretched, admitted his guilt; but though he confessed to betraying his friend to the Turanians, he was unable to tell where, in all Turān, Bizhān might be; or, indeed, if he still lived.

It was then almost time for the early summer festival to be celebrated by the Great King, and King of Kings, on behalf of his people, in the temple of Ormuzd. At such a time the Great King might look into a certain sacred cup and see in a vision all that was passing at that very moment in every corner of the world. 'At the festival I shall look into the miraculous cup,' he promised Giv. 'By the grace of Ormuzd, if he lives and is not dead, I shall see where Bizhān is.' Then he ordered that, in the meantime, Gorgin should be cast into prison, under sentence of death, for betraying Bizhān to the Turanians.

At the appointed time, with prayers to Ormuzd, Khosroes looked into the sacred cup and in it he saw Bizhān in Turān, entombed and in chains, weak and worn, but yet alive. Giv and Gudarz were overjoyed; and so, too, was unhappy Gorgin when, in his prison, he heard the tidings.

Khosroes, having considered the matter, said, 'This is no cause for war. Rather, let a brave champion, in the guise of a merchant with his wares, go into Turān with a few companions, and there do what he may to find and free Bizhān. And who braver and better to lead this merchant's caravan than Rustem?'

Rustem, sent for, came at once from Zābulestān and eagerly agreed to Khosroes' plan. He chose out a handful of bold comrades and Khosroes gave them all they needed in the way of goods to sell, costly cloth, and jewellery—ear-rings of lapis lazuli, gems to set in a woman's hair, anklets of silver and bronze, silver pins with heads like the heads of animals—vessels and cups of silver and gold; pottery painted with scenes of men and beasts; lamps of red earthenware fashioned in the shape of an ibex or a gazelle; and fine horse-trappings.

From his prison Gorgin sent to Rustem, begging him to plead with Khosroes for him, asking that, by being one of those who accompanied Rustem into Turān and risked his life for Bizhān's sake, he might in some measure redeem his offence. This Khosroes granted.

When all preparations were completed, Rustem and seven others set out clad as well-to-do merchants; and among the seven, as well as Gorgin, was Rāhām, the son of Gudarz and, therefore, Bizhān's uncle.

In Turān they journeyed slowly, selling their wares and inquiring cautiously after Bizhān as they went; and remaining for several days in each town or city through which they passed, the better to ask their questions and learn, if they might, of Bizhān's fate. When they had reached to only a short distance from Bizhān's prison, Manizha overheard folk speaking of the Persian merchants who had arrived in a nearby town, selling rich merchandise; and, with a hasty farewell to Bizhān, she set off to find them.

Weary and dusty from her long walk, in rags and no longer beautiful, on reaching the place where the supposed Persian merchants were lodged, she asked to speak with their leader, and, after much argument, was finally taken to Rustem. 'You have lately come from Persia,' she said to him. 'What tidings have you of the family of Gudarz? What of young Bizhān? Do his father Giv and his grandfather Gudarz search for him? He lies in fetters a few leagues from here. I beg of you, send a message to Giv and Gudarz and tell them of it.'

At first Rustem did not trust her; he feared that he and his supposed brother-merchants were suspected of being what they really were, and that this young woman had been sent to lead them into a trap. 'Woman,' he said, 'I know naught of Gudarz and Bizhān. I am neither a great lord nor a warrior, but only an honest merchant, so the family of Gudarz is as nothing to me. Begone.'

But Manizha persisted in her appeals, with tears and on her knees; and in time, by careful questioning, Rustem learnt who she was and where Bizhān was imprisoned. When he knew she was to be trusted, he told her both, that he was Rustem, and why he and his companions had journeyed into Turān. Then, bidding her return to Bizhān and make ready a beacon fire to guide them, he promised to come with his comrades on an appointed night, to free Bizhān.

Overjoyed, Manizha hastened back to Bizhān with her happy tidings. Together—together in their hearts, though their bodies were separated by a slab of rock—they awaited the moment of their deliverance. When the time was come, Manizha set fire to the pile of brushwood and sticks which she had gathered.

Guided by this beacon, Rustem and his companions came to her. While Rustem sent keen glances all about him into the darkness, to make sure they had not been discovered or followed, the other seven champions laid their hands upon the slab of stone which covered Bizhān's prison. But not one hair's breadth could they move it. They called for help to Rustem and, coming hastily, alone he raised the huge stone, lifted it high above his head and cast it a great distance away. Manizha marvelled at it; as did Gorgin, Rāhām, and the other five, for, though the full extent of Rustem's strength was not unknown to them, as it was to Manizha, they still reckoned it a wonder to see him lift so easily a block of stone which they had not been able to shift.

Then, with ropes they raised Bizhān, pale and thin, from the pit and struck off his chains. He and Manizha, weeping tears of joy, flung their arms about each other. Gorgin fell at Bizhān's feet, imploring his forgiveness; and in his happiness at his liberation and at being restored to the side of Manizha, Bizhān was unable to deny anything to any man. Besides, he considered, had it not been for Gorgin's treachery, he would never have found so fond and so constant a wife.

Before they returned to Persia, Rustem and his comrades decided to make a sharp night attack upon the palace of Afrāsib. Accordingly, on the chosen evening, when darkness had fallen, casting off their merchants' guise and appearing as the armed warriors that they were, they fell upon the palace gates, cutting down the guards and all who would have prevented them. Rustem, on Raksh, rode into the palace at the head of the others, pressing forward eagerly and crying, 'Where are you, Afrāsib, you who ever deal so harshly with the husbands of your daughters? Here is Rustem, son of Zāl, come to seek you out.'

Afrāsib, taken quite by surprise, did not wait to see his men face their attackers. Not for the first time in his life, he fled from his palace by a postern gate in the darkness, leaving the Persians triumphant.

20: The Departure of Khosroes

THE capture of the Emperor Afrāsib's palace by Rustem and the seven champions was the beginning of a renewal of open warfare between the two empires, Persia and Turān. The struggle was long, cruel, and bitter, but it seemed that Ormuzd favoured the Persians, for theirs was victory after victory. On a day of sorrow for the Turanians, their commander-in-chief, good old Pirān, was slain, and Persia had lost its noblest enemy. Sincerely mourned by all, the old man was given a burial worthy of a warrior and a hero, with all the honour and respect that he had earned in his long life of service to his land. And there was no one who, on hearing of the death of Pirān, doubted that his most virtuous spirit—when once it had crossed the bridge of the dead—would have flown upwards past the stars and beyond the moon and the sun, to be received for ever into the infinite light of Ormuzd.

Time after time Afrāsib fled before the triumphant progress of the Persians who were led into battle—once the final victory seemed certain to be theirs—by the Great King Khosroes himself. And then at last there came a day when Afrāsib's flight was too long delayed, or else not swift enough, and he was taken captive by the rejoicing Persian army. Khosroes, on being told the tidings, ordered that Afrāsib should be brought before him.

Seeing the younger monarch look at him with hatred in his glance as he strode towards him, a drawn sword in his hand, Afrāsib remembered his old dream, dreamt before Khosroes' birth, and he thought, 'So at last it is to come true, that nightmare, the memory of which has plagued me so often in the past.' His heart sank with dread and bitterly he regretted that he had followed the merciful counsel of Pirān, on that day when Khosroes, seeming only a half-witted shepherd lad, had stood before him to be questioned. Yet aloud he said to Khosroes, haughtily and with contempt, 'Wretch, would you slay your grandfather?'

'You slew my father Siyāvush,' retorted Khosroes. 'You slaughtered him as a butcher would slaughter an ox.'

Bitterly they accused and cursed each other and cast taunts and words of hatred like weapons. All their imperial dignity forgotten, they were no more than two enemies, one old and the other of middle years, who stood face to face again at last and spoke with no dis-

sembling. And in the end, in spite of Afrāsib's furious protests of his kinship with his captor, Khosroes struck off his head, and with that stroke became overlord of all Turān. Yet for all his hatred, he permitted Afrāsib a funeral that was fitting for an emperor.

Khosroes sent word of Afrāsib's death to old Kāvus, where he lived quietly in his retirement from the world, and the old man gave thanks to Ormuzd that Siyāvush was finally avenged. Then he said to himself, 'I have lived to see vengeance, therefore I have lived long enough. I await nothing now, save death.' And soon afterwards he died.

For forty days Khosroes mourned his grandfather and then there began for Persia the festivities with which were celebrated the great victory over Turān. In thankfulness for his triumph, Khosroes freed all captive Turanians and permitted them to return to their homes. He ordered that all subject-kings who had owed allegiance to Afrāsib, and even Afrāsib's successor himself, should pay their tribute-money to Persia and be vassals of the Great King, and King of Kings, for all future days. Then, believing that thus there would be peace between the two empires in the years to come, Khosroes, wearied, declared his work to be done and named as his successor Lohrāsp, another grandson of Kāvus; and, in spite of the protests and entreaties of his courtiers and his champions, his counsellors and his warriors, he bade farewell to his subjects and his family and went alone to the mountains. As his mourning people, standing at a distance, with tears watched him climb upwards, a sudden snowfall hid him from their sight. When it was past and the mountains were clearly to be seen once more, Khosroes had vanished, and no man saw him ever again.

21: Gushtāsp

THE Great King Lohrāsp had two sons, Zarir and Gushtāsp, both clever and valiant young men, who alike, in skill at arms and in all other ways, far surpassed their father. Of the two, Lohrāsp preferred Zarir and ever favoured him with lavish gifts and high offices; but for Gushtāsp he cared little and on him he bestowed nothing. For many years Gushtāsp bore this patiently; but at last there came a day when he could endure it no longer. One pleasant spring evening, as Lohrāsp feasted in the palace gardens with his courtiers and his two sons, all seated beneath the blossom-laden trees, in the sight and hearing of every man there, Gushtāsp rose and addressed his father.

'Great King, may Ormuzd bless and ever keep you. You are the mighty ruler of two empires and I, your son, am no more than a slave at your feet. Yet, in the giving of counsel I am no fool, in courage I am the equal of any man, and in deeds of arms I believe myself surpassed by few. Great King, even as Khosroes named you his successor, I ask you, in like manner, to name me, your son Gushtāsp, as the one who is to wear the imperial tiara when you are gone—may that sad day be far from us.'

After a moment Lohrāsp replied, 'My son, you are over-eager, which is a fault in one so highly born. Be patient and consider this: through every garden there runs a channel of water for the refreshment of the flowers which grow there. In the early spring, when the mountain snows melt and descend to the valleys, even a little garden stream may swell to a flood and damage or destroy the plants which it was dug to serve. Remember this, and seek no longer to enlarge yourself beyond your due!'

Gushtāsp, remembering instead all the many favours and offices with which his brother was ever being enlarged, grew angry. 'Great King, if you have neither love nor kindness to spare for your own son, it were as well that he sought both in some other place than your court.' And with that he left his father and his father's guests; and that very night he rode from the palace, quite alone.

For many months he wandered from land to land; until at last he left behind all those kingdoms which made up the two empires of Persia and Turān, and came to the empire of the Lands of the West, ruled from the great city of Rome by the Caesar, a descendant of

Salm, that son of Feridun to whom his father had given the lands that lay to the west of the world.

Rome was not only a large city, it was also beautiful, and rich with many marvels; and it pleased Gushtāsp, so that he determined to remain in Rome for a time. He found lodgings in the city and then he sought employment, since the little gold he had brought with him when he left his father's palace, was almost spent.

He went first to a scrivener, to whom he said, 'Sir, I am a scribe and I have journeyed from Persia to your city, for it is in Rome that I wish to dwell. If you would take me as your assistant, you would not find me unskilled.'

The scrivener looked at Gushtāsp's straight limbs and his strong hands and said, 'Your body was fashioned to wear armour, not the robe of a scribe; and your hands were formed to hold a sword, not a pen. There is no need of your services here.'

Gushtāsp shrugged his shoulders and went to a horse-dealer. 'Sir,' he said, 'I can ride as well as any other man, and I can break in any colt that was ever foaled. You would find it of profit to you, were you to hire me to have charge of your herds.'

'I have no reason to doubt that you speak truly, stranger,' replied the horse-dealer. 'Yet I would be a great fool to give charge of any part of my herd to one on whom I never set eyes before this day, and who might well be a horse-thief, or worse.'

Gushtāsp sighed and went next to a camel-driver. 'I ask no wages of you, sir,' he said. 'For my keep alone I ask a place among those who serve you and drive your camel-trains.'

The camel-driver looked long and closely at Gushtāsp before he said, 'You have the air of a high-born man—the air, even, of a prince. I am a simple camel-driver, I could not offer employment to such a one as you.'

Dispirited, Gushtāsp went to a smithy. 'Sir,' he said to the smith, 'I am young and strong. Give me work, and I can promise that you will find me willing.'

The smith looked at Gushtāsp's broad shoulders and his strong arms. He nodded. 'I will take you as my apprentice when you have shown me that you have strength enough for the hard work of a smithy.' And he ordered his assistants to take from the furnace a large ball of iron and lay it on the anvil. He then handed Gushtāsp a heavy iron hammer and bade him, if he could, make of the white-hot ball a flat disc.

Gushtāsp raised the hammer while the smith and his men looked on. With his first blow he not only flattened the iron ball, he also split the anvil asunder.

The smith's assistants gaped in admiration; but the smith said, 'Away with you, and fast, young man. There is no place here for one who, in no time at all, would wreck my whole smithy.'

Gushtāsp threw down the hammer and, near to desperation, went from the smithy, wondering where he would sleep that night, and if he would eat that day. Miserably he walked through the streets of Rome and out through one of its gates. Beyond the wall, near to the gate, there grew a shady tree; and here he sat down, his head in his hands, and pondered over what was to become of him.

One of the elders of Rome, a good and kindly old man whose house stood in the pleasant countryside a short distance from the city, passing by on his way home, saw Gushtāsp and stopped to say to him, 'Young man, you seem to have a private grief. If it would ease your heart a little, come with me to my house, where you may rest and eat—and speak of your troubles, if you will.'

Gratefully Gushtāsp went with the old man and remained in his house, an honoured guest, for many days. He told his host no more of himself than that he was a Persian, and he called himself Farukzād.

Now, at that time while Gushtāsp was in the house of his benefactor, one of the Caesar's daughters, Katāyun, reached the age at which she might be wed; and the Caesar called to his palace at an appointed time, all the elders of Rome, that she might choose a husband from among them. When they were assembled together, he sent for Katāyun. She came, accompanied by her maidens, and walked about the hall looking in turn at each of the men gathered there. When she had seen every one of them, her father asked her, 'Have you made your choice, my daughter?'

She shook her head. 'No, lord father, for I have seen here today no man whose wife I would be.'

The Caesar dismissed the elders, bidding them seek out and send to the palace on the following day, all young men of rank and fortune, that Katāyun might make her choice from among them.

When Gushtāsp's host returned from the palace, he told Gushtāsp of the day's events and asked him, 'Tomorrow, why should you not go to the palace and take your place among the young men who seek the hand of the princess?'

'I am poor, and a foreigner in your land,' said Gushtāsp. 'What hope have I of marrying the Caesar's daughter?'

'You may be poor,' said the old man, 'and of your birth and rank I know nothing. Yet for seemly and honourable conduct, no prince could surpass you; in strength and feats of arms you would be the match of any Roman warrior; and in form and feature you are such a man as might please even a princess.'

So, encouraged by his host, the next morning Gushtāsp presented himself at the palace along with the young noblemen of Rome and waited with them in the hall for the princess to come and make her choice. But whereas all the others there waited proudly and boldly in the centre of the hall, where they might be seen to the best advantage in all their splendid garments and their jewels, Gushtāsp, simply and poorly clad, and without a single jewel, stood by himself in a corner of the hall, apart from the others and as though he were not one of Katāyun's suitors—and this that he might not see the scorn and hear the mockery of those other, rich, young men.

When Katāyun came with her maidens, she moved about the hall, looking first at one and then at another of the hopeful or confident young men gathered there; and as she glanced at him, each one thought, 'It is I.' But she passed by every one of them until she had looked upon all save Gushtāsp; and she still had not made her choice. She sighed, for she had seen no man whom she could love, and she asked her maidens, 'Have I seen them all?'

Someone answered her, 'Dear mistress, you have seen them all, save one who stands yonder, in the corner. Yet he is poorly dressed and no fit suitor for a princess.'

'Nevertheless,' said Katāyun, 'I will see him, since he has come here with the others.'

She went to where Gushtāsp waited with downcast eyes; for, prince that he was, he was proud and so he dreaded to see her contempt. But she stood for many moments watching him, and all the while a smile grew upon her lips and in her lovely eyes. And then she said, 'This is he whom I choose for my husband.' And taking off the crown she wore, she set it on Gushtāsp's head.

When the Caesar learnt that his daughter had chosen for her husband a young foreigner who had neither riches nor, it seemed, rank, to make him acceptable, he was angry and bade her choose again, and more fittingly. And when she refused to do his bidding, he said furiously, 'Then you may marry this pauper whom you have chosen, but you need expect no blessing of mine and no dowry. Nor will your husband or his wife ever be welcome at my court.'

So, against the Caesar's wishes, Gushtāsp and Katāyun were wed; and once again Gushtāsp's kindly host showed himself a good friend, giving them both a home under his hospitable roof.

After a few years, when Gushtāsp had proved himself by his deeds to be, although a foreigner and, apparently, of lowly birth, a young man to be reckoned with and one who wished Rome well and was ready to risk his very life for his adopted land, the Caesar forgave Katāyun and received her once again at court, and Gushtāsp with her; and so they dwelt happily in the Caesar's favour for some time.

But there came a day when the Caesar in Rome, like many a ruler before him—and many and many another who was to come after—looked with greedy eyes upon other lands, and it seemed to him that it would be a fine thing to rule the whole world, east and west, as Feridun, his ancestor, had done. 'All the subject-kings of Persia—and, now, of Turān, likewise—pay tribute to the Great King Lohrāsp,' he thought. 'Therefore, if Lohrāsp himself paid tribute to Rome, then all the world would be mine to command.' And he sent a messenger to Lohrāsp, demanding tribute and threatening war if payment were refused.

At first the Great King Lohrāsp was uncertain as to how he should reply, for he knew the Caesar's power to be very great and his army very large, and he had no mind to bring a long and terrible war upon the people of his two empires. But at last he decided to resist and he sent his son Zarir, with an escort of picked warriors and the Banner of Kāva fluttering above them, with his reply to the Caesar: 'Let it be war.'

While Lohrāsp had been considering his answer, the Caesar had left Rome with an army, and with Gushtāsp, as a Persian, at his side to advise him, and he had sailed across the sea and set up his camp on Persian soil, at Aleppo on the coast, believing that the presence of his army in the empire could not fail to hasten Lohrāsp's surrender.

It was therefore to Aleppo, to the camp of the Romans and their allies, that Zarir went with his father's answer to the Caesar's demands; and he came with great pomp and pride into the Caesar's presence. Beside the Caesar, on a lesser throne, sat Gushtāsp. Zarir looked searchingly at Gushtāsp; but as he was garbed in the Roman fashion, and as many years had passed since they had faced one another, Zarir was not sure that the Prince Farukzād was his brother; and Gushtāsp gave him no sign.

The Caesar and Gushtāsp greeted Zarir courteously, and Zarir greeted the Caesar; yet he said no word to the man he suspected might be his brother.

'Why do you not honour my son Farukzād with a greeting?' the Caesar asked.

Zarir hesitated a moment, then he chanced his reply. 'Neither I nor my father the Great King have any greeting for a runaway slave,' he said, and he saw Gushtāsp flush a little, though he bit his lip and said nothing.

The Caesar frowned, not understanding; but he let it pass and demanded, 'Have you brought an answer to my message?'

'I have.'

'And what is that answer?'

'The Great King, and King of Kings, answers the Caesar's demands thus,' said Zarir. 'If the Caesar does not immediately return in peace to Rome, soon it will be the Great King, and King of Kings, who will rule in Rome, as monarch of all the world.'

'The Great King prefers war. So be it,' said the Caesar, and he rose in token that the audience was at an end and that the rulers of Persia and the Lands of the West had no more to say to each other.

With formal words of leave-taking, Zarir went; and the Caesar turned to Gushtāsp and asked, 'You are a man of Persia, and you have told me that you were once at the Great King's court. Why did you not speak to his son, Prince Zarir?'

Gushtāsp did not answer the question, but he said slowly, 'Lord Caesar, I think they want war no more than you want it.' Then, more urgently, he went on, 'I was once respected at the Great King's court and men there will remember me. Lord Caesar, send me to Lohrāsp to speak on your behalf, and this matter may be resolved without weapons.'

To this the Caesar agreed; and Gushtāsp, accompanied by Katāyun, journeyed onward through Persia to the capital, where he presented himself before the Great King. When Lohrāsp saw his son again, and understood how highly the Caesar rated him, he knew at last that he had been wrong to prefer Zarir. That war between Persia and the Lands of the West might be averted, he resigned the tall tiara and the sceptre of Persia to Gushtāsp and retired to the peace of a temple, there to serve Ormuzd as a priest; and the Caesar, satisfied to see the husband of his own daughter upon the imperial throne, made no more demands on Persia.

Gushtāsp ruled well and wisely and did much good for Persia, having also, as had Lohrāsp before him, the overlordship of all Turān. So just a ruler was he, and so great a peacemaker did he prove, that it was said that during his reign a sheep and a wolf might drink together, side by side, from the same pool.

The subject-kings of Persia and Turān—all save Rustem—paid Gushtāsp willing tribute and respected his might. But though Rustem had served Kāvus and Khosroes faithfully, he cared little for Lohrāsp or his sons. He kept from Gushtāsp's court and remained in his own kingdom of Zābulestān and no longer declared himself ready to fight for the sake of Persia, and he paid no tribute-money. For his part, Gushtāsp did not call upon Rustem for service of arms, and he shut his eyes and chose to pretend indifference, that tribute never came to him from Zābulestān. For not only did he believe that Rustem deserved well of Persia for his past deeds for the empire, but also, because though Rustem might have grown older than he had been in his best years, he was an old lion, and his teeth were yet sharp and only a fool would risk a bite from them.

22: Isfendiār

GUSHTĀSP and Katāyun had two sons, Pashutān, a brave and respected general, and the mighty champion Isfendiār, who was second only to Rustem as a hero and a warrior. Isfendiār had many adventures; among them was his battle with the Simurgh, the magical bird who had fostered Zāl. He hunted her down and was said, by men who lived in later years, to have slain her. But, since she was still living at the time of his death, this cannot have been the truth. Yet he must have wounded her sorely and almost to the death; for when he struck her with his sword, he was spattered with her blood all over his body save for his eyes, for those he closed when the blood spurted over him. From that day on, by virtue of the Simurgh's blood, Isfendiār's body became proof against death from all weapons: though he might be wounded by them, he could not be slain, thanks to the magical blood.

The peace of the early days of Gushtāsp's reign did not last for ever. There came a time when Arjāsp, the Emperor of Turān, said to himself, 'I am as great a monarch as the ruler of Persia; my empire is as wide, and I have as many subject-kings as he. Because of a war which Afrāsib lost, why should I pay Gushtāsp tribute for the lands that are rightly mine? Afrāsib is dead, but I am alive, and I will no longer be reckoned a vassal of Gushtāsp.' And against the advice of his counsellors, he refused to pay the tribute-money to Persia, declaring himself the equal of Gushtāsp and, moreover, himself demanding tribute of the Persians.

Once again the two great empires were at war. Leading the Persians against Arjāsp, Zarir was slain. But after Zarir came a far better warrior, his nephew Isfendiār. Eager to avenge his uncle, Isfendiār slew Arjāsp, whose rebellious pride had brought him little gain.

Isfendiār's victories in battle, and his many successful adventures, and the respect which men showed to him, as well as their ceaseless flattery, made him ambitious; and there came a day when he could see no reason why he should not be Great King, and King of Kings, in place of his father Gushtāsp. He went to his mother Katāyun and said, 'When he sent me out against the Emperor Arjāsp, my father promised me, as the prize of victory, the imperial army, the throne, the tiara, and the treasury of Persia. He has forgotten his

promises and he has not yet given me these things. I shall go to him and demand them as my right. If he gives them to me, I will serve him faithfully all his life and be content; but if he refuses me, I will win them by force. He shall then be cast down and I will take his place on the imperial throne as Great King, and King of Kings, and you, my dearest mother, shall be Empress of Persia and rule at my side.'

Katāyun was greatly troubled at her son's words, for she knew that Gushtāsp would never yield to demands and threats: had he not, in his marriage, defied the Caesar and all the Lands of the West? It was unthinkable that he would yield to his own son. 'Dearest Isfendiār,' she said earnestly, 'beloved son, all those things which your father has promised you, will, in time, be yours. Why should you desire his power and his treasury: have you not power enough and treasure in plenty of your own? As for the imperial army, he has given that into your charge by declaring you its commander-in-chief. My Isfendiār, the army you have already, and the other things will be yours one day. Curb your impatience and await that day.'

Isfendiār gave a short laugh and said bitterly, 'There is a saying that only a fool tells his secrets to a woman, since he might as well shout them in the streets. I have no doubt but that you will now go to my father and repeat my words to him.' And in spite of her loving protests, he left her angrily. In this ill mood he shut himself up in his own apartments in the palace and attended his father's court no more.

Gushtāsp guessed his son's ambition to be the cause of his seclusion, and he sent for his counsellor, the wise man Jāmāsp, learned in astrology, and bade him read Isfendiār's destiny in the stars.

When he had cast Isfendiār's horoscope, Jāmāsp began to weep. 'It would have been better had I never been born than that I should have lived to see this day,' he said.

'Come, speak, good Jāmāsp,' urged Gushtāsp. 'What destiny do the stars foretell for my son?'

'Great victories in war, and great renown, and the love and respect of many men,' began Jāmāsp; but Gushtāsp broke in, 'These things I know of already, and they are not matters for tears. Leave his praises unsaid—I have heard them many times—and tell me instead why you weep for my son.'

'I weep for Isfendiār because it is written in the stars that he will die young and at the hands of the only man who surpasses him, the old hero Rustem of Zābulestān.'

Gushtāsp was silent for a time, while Jāmāsp's tears still flowed. Then the Great King said, 'If I were to surrender to Isfendiār all that he desires: my throne, the tiara of Persia, my treasury and the imperial army, surely they would be enough for him and he would be content to leave Rustem in peace? Having all else, surely, as I myself have done, he would forgo the tribute-money from Zābulestān? And if he and Rustem never meet, why then, they cannot fight; and so my son cannot die by Rustem's hand.'

But Jāmāsp still wept. 'No one of us can change what is written in the stars,' he said.

Gushtāsp thought long and deeply on the words of Jāmāsp, and at last he decided to leave the outcome to be what it would, and not seek to alter destiny. If Isfendiār were indeed destined to be slain by Rustem, then, as Jāmāsp had said, no man could prevent it. Yet if Isfendiār were to escape this fate, then it could only be because Rustem had died first and therefore was no danger to the younger man. Yet Rustem, though growing old, had no equal as a warrior —save only, perhaps, Isfendiār himself. Fate must decide between them, Gushtāsp thought to himself. And so when, soon after, Isfendiār came to him and demanded the throne and the tiara, and all that he believed to be rightly his, as a reward for the services he had done for the sake of Persia and his father, Gushtāsp said to him, 'You have indeed performed for me and for the empire all those things of which you have reminded me—and, truly, more than those: your reckoning was too modest. You are the greatest warrior —save one—in all the world, and all Persia bows before you. Yet in Zābulestān old Rustem still lives, and he, your only equal in feats of arms, refuses to acknowledge my claim to the imperial power and he pays us no tribute. As one final task for me, go into Zābulestān and take captive or slay Rustem for the sake of the tribute-money. Then, when your last and only rival is dead or in chains, I will surrender to you all my power: throne, tiara, and treasury shall be yours and you may rule in my place as Great King, and King of Kings. You have my word on it.'

'Rustem may refuse you the tribute-money which he owes,' said Isfendiār. 'Yet he lives in peace and does us no hurt. Why, now and at this time, should the tribute-money from Zābulestān seem a matter of such weight to you, and why should you seek to conquer Rustem except that you thereby expect to endanger my life? Yet I will do as you say. I will go into Zābulestān and challenge Rustem and defeat him. Then I will return to you and demand all that you have promised me.' And while Gushtāsp watched him with divided hopes and feelings, Isfendiār went to make ready to ride for Zābulestān.

23: Rustem and Isfendiār

WITH a small army of chosen warriors, and with his three young sons at his side—Bahmen the eldest and his two younger brothers—Isfendiār rode towards Zābulestān and his destiny.

When they reached a place where the road forked—one path leading to Zābulestān and the other away from Rustem's lands—the camel ridden by the guide who went before them would not take the track which ran towards Zābulestān, but instead it lay down upon the road, and for all his beating and cursing it would not rise.

'This is an ill omen,' Isfendiār's warriors said to him.

'If one stubborn camel is indeed an ill omen,' said Isfendiār, 'then let us destroy it and it will no longer be an omen, either for good or ill.' And he ordered the camel to be slain.

When this had been done, Isfendiār and his men rode on into Zābulestān and reached the River Hirmend without incident, and Isfendiār's spirits rose high and he thought, 'Why should it come to warfare between Rustem and myself? We are the two greatest warriors in all the world and no man is our equal, therefore we should be friends, not foes. Instead of riding upon Rustem with a drawn sword in my hand, I will send to him a message of goodwill.' And he bade his eldest son Bahmen ride on alone to the city of Zābul and ask Rustem to meet him in peace and friendship, there beside the River Hirmend, that they might discuss the Great King's demands with words rather than with blows.

While the others set up their pavilions on the river's bank, young Bahmen was rowed across the water and he set off alone along the road which, a short distance on, climbed up a hill and, on the farther side, ran down into a pleasant valley, where game abounded. At the top of this hill Bahmen looked down and saw on the plain a small hunting-party. At its head, on a huge, golden-yellow, red-dappled horse, rode a man, taller and broader by far than any other Bahmen had ever seen. He carried, as he rode, as well as bow and quiver and hunting spear, a sapling from which he had stripped the leaves and branches, with, impaled upon its end, a wild ass, just as he had run it down and spitted it. Though this man's hair was grizzled and he was not young, yet his limbs were like tree trunks and his muscles showed like iron. 'That will be Rustem, on Raksh,' thought Bahmen, and he began to fear for Isfendiār. So greatly did the boy tremble for his father's safety, should it ever come to combat between him and Rustem, that he dismounted and, dislodging a boulder, he sent it rolling down the hill-side, just as Rustem was riding below him.

Someone, looking upwards, saw the boulder coming and called to Rustem in warning. But though the others in the group all scattered speedily, Rustem, glancing up carelessly at the boulder hurtling down towards him, reined in Raksh and waited. When the boulder was almost on top of him, he drew back one foot in its curving-tipped boot and gave the boulder a little kick which sent it flying across the plain, to land harmlessly, far from him and his companions.

Bahmen, looking on, was appalled; but by now Rustem and the others had seen him at the top of the hill and were calling to him. With as bold and calm an air as he could feign, the boy rode down towards Rustem who greeted him with friendliness and asked his name, for all the world as though he did not know that Bahmen had, not five minutes earlier, sought to murder him.

When Bahmen had given Rustem his father's message, Rustem bade him remain and eat with him while he considered his answer. So, on cushions laid upon the ground, they sat and talked courteously together while the wild ass which Rustem had killed was roasted whole over a fire of glowing logs. Then, when a cloth had been spread upon the ground and dishes and platters and cups set out, with jars of wine and fruit and loaves, the meat, steaming hot from the fire, was brought, and they began to eat. Rustem, in keeping with the needs of his large body, ate and drank hugely and with great enjoyment, and talked much in a good-humoured fashion. But young Bahmen, nervous and apprehensive, lacked appetite. Rustem chaffed him good-naturedly about the little he ate. 'Though you are but young, even here in Zābulestān I have heard much good of the courage and skill at arms of Isfendiār's eldest son. Yet how will you hold and use weapons in time of battle, if you eat no more than a girl could eat?'

Bahmen replied stiffly, 'No one of the imperial line of Persia is a glutton, nor is he a wine-bibber or a prattler.' Yet Rustem only laughed at the boy's discourteous words, as though at a jest.

When the meal was over, Rustem said to Bahmen, 'Go back to your father Isfendiār and tell him that, quite alone, as he desires, I will meet him at the River Hirmend.'

The next day Isfendiār and Rustem met on the banks of the river, one on either side, and spoke together. Isfendiār said, 'I desire no war between us, yet, if you will not submit to my father's demands, there will be no avoiding war. Let you but acknowledge him your overlord and, in token of your surrender, stand before him with your hands in chains, and I will persuade him to instant forgiveness and strike off the chains myself. You will evermore remain high and honoured in the Great King's regard—for how else could he deal with one who has served Persia so long and so well?'

But Rustem answered, 'I will not submit to Gushtāsp. I owe him no allegiance. And no man shall ever see me stand in chains while I still live and breathe. Yet we two can be friends, in spite of your father's enmity. Ride with me now to my palace in my city of Zābul and there remain, an honoured and welcome guest, for as long as you wish. I can offer you rich entertainment for your pleasure, as well as many gifts with which to ride home.'

Isfendiār shook his head. 'That would be to bring down upon me—and rightly—my father's displeasure, that I should become the open friend and guest of one whom he has sent me out to capture and humble. Yet let us instead meet here, upon the plain, and eat and drink together in peace. While I play the host, you shall be my honoured guest.'

Rustem smiled. 'I accept your invitation, Isfendiār. But I have been hunting and my garments are unfitted for a feasting in such noble company. Give me only time enough to return to my palace to bathe myself and change to garb more suited to the occasion. Then, when I return, we may eat and drink and converse like two old friends.'

To this Isfendiār agreed; and when they had decided on an hour for their feasting, for the meantime they parted.

When Rustem returned from Zābul and was rowed across the river, he found Isfendiār's throne set up for him and cushions on the ground for his sons and his followers and guests. Isfendiār received Rustem with ceremony and bade him be seated at his left hand.

But Rustem frowned and said, 'That is not my place. Offer me a place more worthy of my fame.'

'Make ready a place for our guest on my right hand, as he wishes,' Isfendiār bade Bahmen; and the boy rose to obey his father with a resentful glance at Rustem. Isfendiār gestured to Rustem to seat himself on his right hand, but Rustem made no move. He still frowned. 'You may be the son of the Great King of Persia,' he said, 'but my birth is no less high than yours. Am I not the sons' son of kings? Make ready a place more fitting for me, Isfendiār, or I will not sit to eat with you.'

And so Isfendiār had to order that a throne like his own, gilded and spread with rich cloth, should be set up opposite his; and then, at last, Rustem seated himself. But now he and Isfendiār no longer smiled at each other and their feasting passed uneasily; though, as ever, Rustem ate and drank with relish. And if Rustem had small enjoyment of the company, Isfendiār had none at all; and immediately the eating and drinking were done, Rustem rose to leave.

Isfendiār's anger spilled over in unwise words. 'Boasting of birth and lineage comes but ill from the lips of one who is the son of a demon-born creature, white-haired at his birth and left in the desert to die. I have heard it said of your father Zāl, that the magical Simurgh bird, with whom I have fought, took Zāl to her nest as meat for her brood. But even they turned aside from demon-begotten flesh; and so your father survived, growing tall and strong on the scraps of carrion which the Simurgh's fledglings rejected.'

'My father Zāl is the son of Sām and not the child of a demon,' said Rustem furiously. 'It is true that I come of the line of Zohāk the monster on my mother's side, but that is all for which any man may reproach me. As for your line, of which you are so proud, had it not been for my loyalty and my strong arms and all that I performed for Kāvus and Khosroes, there would have been no imperial throne, no tiara, no treasury—and no Persia—for your father's father to take as a gift.'

'Your deeds performed for Kāvus and Khosroes are old tales now,' said Isfendiār. 'It is your defiance of my father Gushtāsp which concerns us today. And these are my last words upon the matter: either you ride with me tomorrow and submit to my father, or we meet in battle at dawn. And whatever your choice, the end will be the same, whether you submit like a coward to be punished or fight like a fool to be defeated. Whatever your choice, you will stand in chains before the Great King, and King of Kings.'

Rustem gave an exclamation of scorn. 'Old Rustem will stand in chains before no man alive, little prince. Tomorrow the two of us, in single combat, without our men, shall meet to try the truth of our boasting. And beware what befalls you in the morning, Isfendiār!' And gesturing to his followers, he turned and left Isfendiār. Yet in his mind he was troubled, thinking, 'Either way this matter will end to my disadvantage. If I am slain or made captive, whatever my former deeds, men will remember only my ending, that I was worsted and shamed by young Isfendiār. And if I slay him, however mighty—warrior or demon—were those I fought against and conquered in former days, men will remember of me only that I, the elder and world-famed champion, took advantage of Isfendiār's fewer years.' Thus thought Rustem, disregarding all that other men said of Isfendiār, that in strength and battlecraft he was second only to Rustem, son of Zāl—second to Rustem as Rustem had been in his former prime and his best days.

At dawn of the next day, both Rustem and Isfendiār made ready, putting on their armour and choosing their weapons. When all was prepared, Rustem, mounted on Raksh, led his men to the River Hirmend; then, bidding them, no matter how much they were provoked, to remain on that side of the river, he alone crossed over and called out his challenge to Isfendiār. Isfendiār, also, forbade his men to fight. 'The outcome of this matter of the tribute-money from Zābulestān shall be decided by Rustem and by me alone,' he said.

They met on a level stretch of ground beside the river, while the men of Zābulestān and Isfendiār's followers and his sons looked on. First they thrust at each other with their long spears until the armour of both was dented and their spear-heads broke. They flung away the useless shafts then, and drew their huge swords. Charging and counter-charging and hewing with strokes each mighty enough to bring down a tree, they blunted the edges of their swords until the once-sharp weapons held no more danger than the wooden toys of a child. Then they cast aside their swords and each man took hold of the heavy battle-mace which hung from his saddlebow. For long and weary hours they fought; and as they fought, striking and dodging the other's strokes, each realized that, in the other, he had met his most worthy adversary. Had Isfendiār truly been the matchless warrior men believed him, he would have slain Rustem without too much toil; and had it not been that Rustem was no longer young and that Isfendiār had bathed in the Simurgh's blood, Isfendiār would have lain lifeless in the dust before an hour's fighting had passed.

At length their battle-maces were cracked and split and they dropped them down. Now they had no more weapons left and only their strong bodies with which to fight. Both men, bruised and fast tiring, were bleeding from a score of wounds; and Raksh also, and Isfendiār's horse, were wounded and spent. As again and again they forced their weary mounts into a gallop close beside one another,

Isfendiār and Rustem leant inwards and caught at each other's belt, each seeking to drag the other towards him and unhorse him and fling him to the ground. But their strength was equal and neither could gain an advantage, though they tried time after time, galloping first in one direction and then wheeling round to gallop in another, until both men and horses were almost unable to endure a moment longer.

While their fight went on, that which both the champions had feared came to pass: their followers joined battle. At first it was no more than a few hot-headed men from either side who, excited by their leaders' deeds, crossed the river, shouting insults and threats and flourishing their weapons. Then suddenly two of them fell to fighting; and two more; and then, seeing their comrades in danger, from each side more and more men splashed forward and joined in, and soon there was a battle between them all. Rustem and Isfendiār, intent as they were on their own combat, saw, too late to prevent it, what had taken place; and each in his heart blamed the other for breaking faith and ordering his men to battle. Yet so paramount was their own mortal combat, that it seemed to them only a small matter when their followers fought; until a man came running to Isfendiār with the tidings that his two younger sons, who had been standing before the front rank of his men to watch their father slay Rustem, had, when the fighting began so suddenly, been caught between the two armies, and had been struck down and were dead.

Isfendiār cried out in his grief and cursed Rustem as a murderer of children. In his anger he forgot his weariness. His desire for revenge strengthened his arm and he attacked once again as though he were only at that moment come to combat. With Rustem it was otherwise. Shocked by the senseless cruelty of the deed, his resolve weakened by the fact that it had been in his name that two young boys had been slaughtered, he called back to Isfendiār, protesting his innocence and swearing truly that he had given no orders for an attack.

Thus it was with the news which had brought fresh vigour and fresh hatred to Isfendiār, there came to Rustem only an even greater weariness than he already felt, and a distaste for further fighting. He still defended himself from Isfendiār's renewed and violent assault; but he made no attacks himself. Both badly wounded, he and Raksh fell back before Isfendiār's fury as evening drew close; and finally, turning Raksh's head, Rustem retreated on to a mountain pathway, and so rode home to Kābul, leaving to Isfendiār the victory in that day's fighting.

To his friends and followers, and to his father Zāl, Rustem said, 'Today I barely escaped with my life. Isfendiār is maddened by wrath and grief, I cannot survive another day against him. If I return to the fighting at the rising of tomorrow's sun, it will be the last dawn that I shall look upon.'

All who heard him looked grave, and many wept. But old Zāl—whose white hair was now fitted to his age and no longer seemed strange in any way—said, 'It is said there is a cure for every ill, save only death; and a way out of every difficulty but dying. Yet I will find a means to save you, my son.' He took from the folds of the piece of cloth where it had lain for many years, the Simurgh's feather which she had given him on the day of Rustem's birth, and he burnt it on a brazier. Instantly, as at the birth of Rustem, her black shadow fell on everything; and then the room grew slowly light again, and there was the Simurgh, folding her vast wings.

'What would you of me, Zāl, my fosterling?' she asked.

'Heal my son Rustem and Raksh his horse,' pleaded Zāl. 'And give him the strength and the cunning to slay Isfendiār.'

Plucking out a dark wing-feather with her beak, the Simurgh passed it over the wounds of both Rustem and Raksh, and instantly they were healed and whole again. 'As for Isfendiār,' she said, 'he who slays Isfendiār can expect naught but ill from it and no long years to follow. It were best, son of my foster-child, that you sought peace with Isfendiār and his pardon for the death of his sons, when you next meet with him. Yet, lest he deny you forgiveness, I will give you the weapon by which alone he may be slain.' Then, bidding Rustem follow her, the Simurgh flew slowly from the palace into the darkness, while Rustem, on Raksh, followed her flying shape, darker even than the night, for many leagues until they reached the seashore. There she alighted and showed Rustem a tamarisk bush whose feathery-leaved branches stood tall and straight. The Simurgh passed her wings over Rustem's head in blessing and bade him cut an arrow-shaft from the tamarisk; and he obeyed her, using his dagger to cut a long branch.

'The arrow formed from this wood will be Isfendiār's fate,' she said. 'Shape it and straighten it and harden it carefully in the fire. Fix to it three feathers—no more and no less. Then find two old and well-tested arrow-heads, sharpen them and fashion a double-headed arrow. Then, if tomorrow Isfendiār refuse the peace you ask, set this double-headed arrow to your bow and aim for his eyes, and for no other spot. Now farewell to you, son of my son.' And she spread wide her black wings and was gone.

Rustem rode swiftly back through the night with the tamarisk branch. In his palace, he fashioned from it a double-headed arrow, as the Simurgh had bidden him; and by dawn he was ready and armed, and it was time for him to ride out to meet Isfendiār once more.

Again those two who were the greatest warriors in the world and had no equals, faced each other in the early morning light.

At once Isfendiār, still grieving bitterly for the death of his children, called out across the distance of fifty paces or so which separated them, 'In spite of your wounds, have you lived to see this day, my enemy? Truly you have been healed of your hurts by some evil magic of Ahrimān, else would you be lying dead at this moment. Yet think not that, because you have survived the night, you have escaped my vengeance. Your death has but been delayed. Today shall be your last.'

In obedience to the Simurgh's command, Rustem laid no hand upon his weapons, and he called back to Isfendiār, requesting peace. 'I have not come out to meet you today in combat, but to ask your pardon that it was for my sake, yet through no will of mine, that your two sons were slain. Grant me your forgiveness for that offence, for I am innocent of it. Let there be a truce between us. Come with me to my palace in peace and as my guest and, after, I will ride with you to the Great King as a free man and surrender myself to his mercy.'

'There can be no truce between us,' Isfendiār retorted. 'If you ride with me to my father, it will be as a prisoner, in chains.'

'When he seeks peace with you, you should not speak thus to Rustem, who was a great champion and renowned through all the world many years before you were born, Isfendiār. You should not speak thus to Rustem lest, to your cost, you anger him. Yet once more I ask you, Isfendiār: let me go with you to the Great King unfettered and of my own will, and I shall give you jewels from my treasury, and slaves without number—I will even bid the best of the warriors of Kābulestān follow you and serve you with the strength of their arms, if only you will permit me to go into the Great King's presence at your side and surrender myself to him.'

'Do you seek to bribe me, Rustem? Come, I grow impatient. The choice is yours. Which is it to be: war or chains?'

Rustem sighed. 'Since you will not listen to my pleading, it must be war.' But still he made no move to attack and waited for Isfendiār to be the first to strike.

After a few moments Isfendiār shouted scornfully, 'You have chosen war, yet it seems you lack the valour to act upon your choice.

Make speed and come nearer, Rustem, for I grow weary of waiting to laugh at your death.' Isfendiār, his eyes full of hatred, laid his hand upon his bow, as though he would have shot at Rustem from where he was.

Slowly Rustem took the double-headed arrow from his quiver and set it to his bow, still hoping that Isfendiār might relent while there was yet time.

'You have lived too long, Rustem,' Isfendiār taunted him. 'You have lived too long if you have lived until the day when you go reluctantly to battle.'

'Great Ormuzd,' Rustem prayed, 'you have seen how I tried for peace and was offered only war. Be with me now and forgive me if I offend.' He loosed the two-headed arrow straight at Isfendiār's eyes, shining darkly and flashing in anger, below his helmet. Rustem's aim was true, and with an arrow piercing deeply through each eye, Isfendiār fell with a cry from his horse; and his warriors ran to his side.

Slowly Rustem rode towards his dying rival. He dismounted and men made way for him until he could look down on Isfendiār whose followers tried vainly to fight off his death, while Bahmen wept on the ground beside his father.

'Are you there, Rustem?' asked Isfendiār. 'I cannot see, but I feel your presence near me.'

'I am here, Isfendiār.'

'Now, once again, there will be no one to dispute your claim to be the greatest warrior in the world.'

'We two,' said Rustem, 'should have fought together, side by side, against the enemies of Persia.'

Isfendiār's voice grew weaker as he spoke. 'The time for bitterness is past,' he said. 'And I would wish my son Bahmen to learn all he may of battle-craft from the greatest warrior in the world. I shall soon be dead, Rustem, so it is you who must instruct my son for me. I want no lesser man to guide his steps to manhood. You owe it to me, Rustem, since it was in your name that his two brothers were slain.'

'Do not fret yourself,' said Rustem. 'I will watch over Bahmen and teach him all I know, even as I watched over and taught young Siyāvush.'

'It is well,' Isfendiār whispered. And, not long after these last words, he died.

He was mourned much and deeply by all Persia; though the

Great King Gushtāsp was, in his heart, not sure whether he was glad or sorry that his ambitious son was dead. Certainly, he did not long blame Rustem for Isfendiār's death; and later he and Rustem were reconciled and met as friends. As for Bahmen, in time he succeeded his grandfather as Great King, and King of Kings.

24: The Death of Rustem

ZĀL had a son, many years younger than Rustem, born to him of a slave-girl. His father had named him Sheghād and sent him, as a child, to be trained in the arts of war and peace by the then king of Kābulestān, who was Zāl's kinsman by his marriage to Rudāba. Sheghād grew to be a handsome young man, of pleasing manners and persuasive in speech. He was high in the confidence of the king of Kābulestān, who gave him his daughter in marriage. Both Sheghād and his friend the king were envious of Rustem's fame, and in their hearts they both longed to see his downfall. They talked together much of their desire and dreamt dreams of a world without Rustem. And thus, fed by words and hopes, their desire grew until it was so heavy they could no longer bear to carry it, and they plotted together to bring about the death of Rustem, that they might be eased of their burden. They planned to feign to quarrel openly, so that Sheghād would have a reason for going to Rustem and asking his help in avenging the slights and insults put on him by the father of his wife. Sheghād was to persuade Rustem to go alone to Kābul, where the king was to humble himself and ask forgiveness, and request that Rustem, in token of pardon, would remain with him as his guest for a day or so. Then the king was to invite Rustem out hunting and lure him into a trap; and so, under the guise of an unfortunate mishap, cause his death.

When all had been decided upon and arranged to their satisfaction, the king of Kābulestān made a great feasting to which all his counsellors and lords were invited. During this feasting, Sheghād, feigning drunkenness, rose to his feet and began boasting in a loud voice. When he was sure that all present were listening to him, he cried out, 'In whatsoever company I honour by my presence, I am the noblest and most renowned, for is not great Rustem my brother? What is the worth of our host, the king of Kābulestān, beside the worth of the brother of Rustem?'

The king pretended to fly into a great rage. He leapt up and retorted, 'Any claim to renown which you have, Sheghād, is in being the unworthy husband of my daughter. You call yourself Rustem's brother. What is that but idle boasting and lies? Your mother was no more than a slave-girl. For all that Zāl acknowledged you as his son, how do you know that your father was not another slave?'

'Rustem shall hear of this and avenge your insults to his brother,' shouted Sheghād. He turned his back on the king and walked away, apparently overcome by anger. He rode at once from the city of Kābul, and going to Rustem in Zābulestān, told him of the king's open insults and asked Rustem to avenge him. 'If you do but go alone into Kābulestān and threaten him, my brother, he will come crawling to your feet, trembling, for he is a coward as well as a liar. It would be a heartwarming sight to me, to see him in the dust,' said Sheghād.

So Rustem, on Raksh, rode into Kābulestān, with only a servant or two, and no warriors; and Sheghād followed close after him, rejoicing that, so far, the wicked plan was succeeding.

As Rustem approached the city of Kābul, word of his coming was carried to the king by a swift messenger from Sheghād; and the king immediately set out to meet Rustem on the road. There, bareheaded and barefooted, he knelt in the dust until Rustem reached him. Then, with pretended tears and false repentance, he humbled himself and begged Rustem's forgiveness for his insults to Sheghād. 'Mighty Rustem,' he finished, 'grant me your pardon and implore your brother, also, to pardon me. I will give him riches and gifts, and even, if you bid it, give up my throne to him.'

Rustem, deceived, said, 'Keep your throne and your riches. My brother will, I am certain, forgive you your foolish talk, even as I do. Come, now, rise and greet me in a fashion better suited to the dignity of a king.'

Rejoicing in his evil heart, the king asked that Rustem would honour his palace and remain in Kābul as his guest for a day or so. 'The hunting here is good,' he said. 'I can promise you fine sport, and game well worth your skill.'

Rustem cheerfully agreed to this, and the next day they rode out to the hunt, Rustem, the king, Sheghād, and many courtiers. At the king's suggestion they rode along a certain path where the king had prepared his traps: many deep pits dug and lined with sharpened stakes and blades and covered over with branches and a thin layer of soil and reeds.

By signs known only to themselves, the king of Kābulestān and Sheghād were careful to avoid the pits; but they so managed matters that Rustem, on Raksh, was persuaded straight along the track ahead of them. At first the way was wide enough and Raksh, smelling the freshly-dug soil, was suspicious and skirted the first pits safely. But after, when the path narrowed between the thick undergrowth and trees, there was no avoiding the pits, if a man were to ride forward at all.

Midway between two pits, Raksh stopped dead, ears laid back, nostrils snuffing at the scent of the earth and the cut branches, and every muscle stubbornly resisting Rustem's urging. At first Rustem only wondered at the strange behaviour of Raksh, thinking that perhaps he had some good reason for his refusal to take that path; and he tried with encouraging words, with hands and heels, to coax Raksh on; but the great golden-yellow horse stood like a rock. Such was the friendship between man and beast that Raksh might well have saved Rustem from Sheghād's hatred and treachery; but Rustem was stung by the laughter of the king and his courtiers, and by their mockery as they jested about how little it availed one to own the most famed horse in the world, if one were not man enough to master him; and he lost his temper and called for a whip. Then, lashing furiously at Raksh and shouting at him, he tried to force him onward. Still Raksh would not move forward a single step; but under the blows of the whip he reared up, neighing shrilly, stepping backwards from the danger which lay before him. And so it was that he stepped backwards towards the danger which lay behind. One hoof trod upon the light branches that covered the pit, and in an instant he had overbalanced and he and Rustem had dropped into the trap, their bodies pierced by a score of blades and sharp-pointed stakes.

Rustem at first thought only that some unexpected mishap had befallen him and Raksh; and then he saw the eager face of Sheghād, peering down over the edge of the pit, and he knew the truth. 'Wretch,' he cried, 'you have slain your brother, who never did you harm.'

Sheghād laughed. 'You have slain many men in your time, brother, men who had done you no harm.'

'That was ever in fair fight,' said Rustem. 'I was no murderer.'

The king of Kābulestān dismounted and stepped to the edge of the pit. He was a less honest villain than his daughter's husband, and he ever believed in caution. He now pretended surprise and distress. 'Great Rustem,' he exclaimed, 'what unhappy misfortune is this that has come to you? Yet do not despair, my men will fetch ropes and I shall send for my best physicians. Soon we will have you safely out from this pit and in their healing care.'

Rustem replied to him bitterly, 'I know, even as you know, that the ropes will be brought too late. And not all the physicians in the

world can heal me now. You may spare yourself the labour of wringing tears from eyes which shine with joy. I am as good as dead, and you know it.'

Drawing breath with difficulty, and clenching his teeth against the pain of his many deep wounds, Rustem looked up again at Sheghād. At the sight, he learnt from his brother's deviousness, and stooped to practise deceit. 'Show yourself a true son of our father, Sheghād. Do not leave your brother here to be torn and devoured alive by the jackals and the kites. String my bow and drop it down to me with my quiver, that I may defend myself against the beasts.' Sheghād did not move, so Rustem went on, 'Drop down my bow, with even a single arrow, that I may defend myself against at least one hungry beast.'

After a moment of further thought, Sheghād called to the huntsman who carried Rustem's bow and quiver. He strung the bow, took one arrow from the quiver, and dropped both down to Rustem. 'Here, brother, catch them. I have done as you asked me, and not much will it avail you, since lions and leopards and jackals are many.' He laughed. 'Shoot straight with your last arrow, my brother.'

Then he saw how Rustem slung the bow over his arm, and with the arrow held between his teeth, aided by the stakes in the pit and digging his fingers into its sides, was dragging his dying body upwards to the mouth of the trap; and Sheghād was suddenly terrified. With a cry he stepped back from the pit, just as Rustem's hands, torn and bleeding, grasped its edge. Sheghād turned and fled for the nearest shelter, a tree which stood close by; and on the farther side of it he stood, pressed against its trunk, his heart beating wildly as he gasped in relief at his narrow escape and cursed himself for having yielded to Rustem's last request. But, in his haste, he had not noticed that the tree behind which he so thankfully hid himself, was old and hollow, though—with a deceit to match his own—it still bore green leaves upon its branches.

Rustem, shuddering with pain, looked over the edge of the pit in time to see Sheghād disappear from his sight behind the tree. His feet balanced on two pointed stakes, his limbs trembling with the effort he was making, Rustem braced himself against the side of the pit to free his hands. His eyes swimming, he took aim with his last arrow. Even his dying strength was greater than that of any other man—though that man had been in his prime and with limbs which were strong and whole.

The arrow found its mark, passing right through the hollow tree and into Sheghād's heart. At the sound of his brother's death-cry, Rustem's lips twisted into a smile, and with a groan he let himself fall back into the pit, on to the stakes beside Raksh. His fingers clenched on Raksh's golden mane. 'Thanks be to great Ormuzd, that my day was not lost in night before I had taken vengeance,' he whispered.

And so died, in the same moment, the greatest of all Persian heroes, Rustem, and his truest friend, Raksh, the best of all horses.

And here, with the end of Rustem, let us, also, make an end of these tales from Firdausi, the poet.